Foundations of Library Services and Programming for Children

Foundations of Library Services and Programming for Children

Lisa Houde

ROWMAN & LITTLEFIELD
Lanham • Boulder • New York • London

Published by Rowman & Littlefield
An imprint of The Rowman & Littlefield Publishing Group, Inc.
4501 Forbes Boulevard, Suite 200, Lanham, Maryland 20706
www.rowman.com

86-90 Paul Street, London EC2A 4NE

Copyright © 2024 by The Rowman & Littlefield Publishing Group, Inc.

All rights reserved. No part of this book may be reproduced in any form or by any electronic or mechanical means, including information storage and retrieval systems, without written permission from the publisher, except by a reviewer who may quote passages in a review.

British Library Cataloguing in Publication Information Available

Library of Congress Cataloging-in-Publication Data

Names: Houde, Lisa, author.
Title: Foundations of library services and programming for children / Lisa Houde.
Description: Lanham : Rowman & Littlefield, 2024. | Includes bibliographical references and index.
Identifiers: LCCN 2024015503 (print) | LCCN 2024015504 (ebook) | ISBN 9781538176832 (cloth) | ISBN 9781538176849 (paperback) | ISBN 9781538176856 (ebook)
Subjects: LCSH: Children's libraries--United States--Administration. | Young adults' libraries--United States--Administration. | Children's libraries--Activity programs--United States. | Young adults' libraries--Activity programs--United States. | Children's libraries--United States. | Young adults' libraries--United States.
Classification: LCC Z718.2.U6 H68 2024 (print) | LCC Z718.2.U6 (ebook) | DDC 025.1/97625--dc23/eng20240510
LC record available at https://lccn.loc.gov/2024015503
LC ebook record available at https://lccn.loc.gov/2024015504

∞™ The paper used in this publication meets the minimum requirements of American National Standard for Information Sciences—Permanence of Paper for Printed Library Materials, ANSI/NISO Z39.48-1992.

Contents

Preface   vii
Acknowledgments   xi

Chapter 1:   The History and Value of Library Services for Children and Foundations in Programming and Childhood Development   1

Chapter 2:   Program Evaluation: Planning for Desired Results   21

Chapter 3:   Storytime and Children's Programming   35

Chapter 4:   The Summer Reading Program   61

Chapter 5:   Services and Resources for Children   75

Chapter 6:   The Welcoming and Inclusive Library   99

Chapter 7:   Intellectual Freedom, Censorship, and Professional Ethics   113

Chapter 8:   Foundations in Administration of Children's Services and Professional Development   121

Chapter 9:   Looking Ahead: What's Next in Library Services for Children   145

Index   155
About the Author   167

Preface

Dear reader, I extend to you a most heartfelt welcome! This was the first sentence in the preface of my first book, *Serving LGBTQ Teens: A Practical Guide for Librarians* (2018), and it is just as genuine a welcome for this second title. Whether you are new to the exciting, challenging, and often just plain fun work of programming for youth from birth to twelve or you are a veteran looking for new ideas, this book has been written for you. Walking tacos, anyone? Does that get your interest? It's one of my favorite programs and creates curiosity in kids; that it involves delicious food doesn't hurt either! That and many other programs, as well as foundational information you need for youth librarianship, can be found in these pages!

Public library programming for children is flourishing! At the writing of this text, I've anecdotally observed an increase in youth traffic at the library where I work as well as in other local libraries. Many of the career positions open to librarians are often within youth services—again, this is observed through the state's listserv. Additionally, courses around children's programming are immediately filled when registration opens at San José State University where I teach children's programming and services as well as other courses; clearly, the need for youth librarians is present and growing. This book provides an updated and, in some areas, a timeless look at services and programming for children. Excellent texts around this topic exist, but many are outdated; this book, as mentioned, will offer a fresh perspective along with current practices.

Foundations of Library Services and Programming for Children will serve as a foundational text for youth librarians—both those currently working in the field seeking to enhance their expertise as well as students seeking to develop a baseline of information about best practices for serving and creating programming for children in the public library.

You'll find the text addresses a wide range of topics, each of which is addressed over nine linear chapters—beginning with an historical perspective of youth services in chapter 1 and culminating in a look forward at potential services that the future may require in chapter 8. The chapters are arranged as follows:

Chapter 1—The History and Value of Library Services for Children and Foundations in Programming and Childhood Development
Providing a look back at historical programming and services for children, this chapter will help the librarian gain a unique perspective that will inform present practices as well as future library offerings for children in programming and services. Technology has changed library services significantly, but a reminder of our roots will help build a strong foundation for today.

Chapter 2—Program Evaluation: Planning for Desired Results
A good program planner begins with the end in mind. Through specific pre-planning for end results as well as reconciling all programming with library strategic plans, the library can ensure that programs presented to the community will, in fact, serve that community's needs. This chapter explores specifics around how to plan programming—seemingly backward!

Chapter 3—Storytime and Children's Programming
At the heart of library service to children is the youth program. In this chapter, I'll deeply explore the penultimate program for children—storytime. Given its prominence, I'll provide a breakdown of storytimes for a variety of age levels and will conclude with general programming and budgeting matters.

Chapter 4—The Summer Reading Program
Second only to storytime in the world of children's programming, summer reading is among the most rewarding programs offered for children—rewarding for both youth and the librarian. I'll examine all facets of summer reading, from planning the program through to the finale, how to connect to schools, and to provide an enriching and fun summer for youth.

Chapter 5—Services and Resources for Children
Among the focuses of this chapter are non-programming services for children. I'll explore readers' advisory for children as well as an historical look at readers' advisory's past. Many folks believe reference services to be ubiquitous with readers' advisory; here, I'll outline the distinctions and explore the values of each. Not to be overlooked, I'll touch on collection development, once the heart and soul of library offerings for children and still vital today. Weeding will be taken up here—it's so important! Finally, I'll explore various methods of shelving children's materials as well as taking a brief look at youth media awards.

Chapter 6—The Welcoming and Inclusive Library
Ensuring that all patrons in your community know they are welcome in the library, in this chapter, I examine space planning, accessibility importance, and equity, diversity, and inclusion in the library. In order to reach the goal of inclusivity, professional development focused exclusively on this topic is critical; this is the final element in the scope of this chapter's content.

Chapter 7—Intellectual Freedom, Censorship, and Professional Ethics
   At the writing of this book, issues around censorship are in the daily news. Looking at intellectual freedom and the librarian's role in assuring the integrity of intellectual freedom will be found here. I'll point out the distinctions between banning, challenging, and censorship, and most importantly, I'll include expert concrete practices for staff dealing with challenges in the library.

Chapter 8—Foundations in Administration of Children's Services and Professional Development
   The administrator of children's services wears many hats. Here, I'll explore core competencies for children's librarians, children's services advocacy, knowledge of digital preparedness for children, and I spend considerable time on management and leadership. Are these two areas the same? Finally, I'll examine the concepts of outreach and marketing.

Chapter 9—Looking Ahead: What's Next in Library Services for Children
   We can only guess, right? Based on past practices and foundations in the field of library services for children, I'll offer some thoughts on what we might expect—and should do to prepare—from and for the future.

I'll wrap up this preface similarly to my first book—it is my sincere hope that you derive benefit from this title, that it inspires you, informs you, and strikes at the heart of youth librarianship's key values. Kids need you.

Acknowledgments

Before anything else, I'd like to thank Rowman & Littlefield for first entertaining the possibility of this book and then accepting the proposal. Special thanks go to Charles Harmon, Erinn Slanina, and Lauren Moynihan—all of whom have been exceptionally wonderful to work with.

A huge thank you to the youth staff at Rye Public Library—you know who you are—who chatted about children's programming with me. Your incredible service to children is noted and deeply appreciated.

To my students who inspire me and push the creativity of children's services in ways I could never imagine; you are incredible people, and the field of librarianship is and will be bettered by your work.

Finally, Sylvia—my spouse. Honestly? You are a ROCK of patience, persistence, and truly are the best at first eyes on my writing; as cliché as it is, this book would not exist without your careful editing and creativity. Thank you, one thousand million times, Syl. Oh, and I can't forget my beloved Moyen poodle Kiki Kenette Min Min Michelline of the Pumpkin House; it's a long name for a beloved tiny friend who was at my side during the entire process of writing this book. Best support ever!

1

The History and Value of Library Services for Children and Foundations in Programming and Childhood Development

Before embarking on a journey into the details of children's services and programming, it's important to look back at where we've been in the library profession—light years away from what's happening in libraries today. If you've been in a library children's department recently, you'll likely have noted a boisterous, engaged, enthusiastic energy; the times of a librarian hiding behind a desk and demanding quiet are long past; so, too, is the librarian who merely connects children with books. Libraries are hubs of community engagement in a variety of formats, and the statistics bear this out. Consider these numbers published in February 2022 and reported by Nicholas Rizzo: In 2019, US libraries held 3.136 million programs for children; this reflects a 21.87 percent increase in programs compared with 2014.[1] Holding more programs doesn't necessarily equate to increased attendance, so here are those numbers as well: 81.84 million kids attended programs in 2019, which is an increase of 16.57 percent from 2014.[2] Pew Research Data published in 2013 on parents, children, and libraries reports that 79 percent of parents consider the library as "very important," and 15 percent surveyed responded that the library is "somewhat important" for their children.[3] That's a whopping 94 percent who see the library as an asset for their children. When looking at statistics focused on children's programming—74 percent of Americans believe it's "very important" for libraries to offer programs and classes, 21 percent indicate programs are "somewhat important," so 95 percent of parents find important value in library programming for their children.[4] Clearly, children's programming is an essential element of library services.

In terms of the types of programming for children, storytime is the most widely offered. Beyond that, librarians have found creative ways through programming to connect children with books, with one another, and with their communities. How did we get here? I'll explore the historical foundation of children's services in brief, and interwoven with this historical information, the value of providing those services to children will clearly be seen. A strong foundation in children's public library services is built from several factors: comprehending what constitutes a library program; establishing a foundation of early literacy and children's developmental stages; and comprehending children's reading development. Along with a look at these elements, I'll examine strategies for librarians later in this chapter.

A BRIEF HISTORY OF CHILDREN'S SERVICES IN THE PUBLIC LIBRARY
THE EARLY DEVELOPMENT OF CHILDREN'S SERVICES

Prior to 1895, services for children were virtually nonexistent within the public library, and certainly no space was designated specifically for children, although it's been noted that the Minneapolis Public Library established a children's room as early as 1893.[5] In fact, as Virginia Walter also notes, "When philanthropists and civic leaders established the first public libraries in the United States in the early 1800s, their intentions were to provide good reading to adults who were not wealthy enough to purchase their own books and to help assimilate immigrants from Europe into American society. With very few exceptions, these early libraries were not open to children."[6] According to Wayne A. Wiegand in *Part of Our Lives: A People's History of the American Public Library*, it wasn't until 1895 that the library profession began to consider directing resources and energy to children; at this time, the mission of the library shifted to include children's services and considerations were made for separate children's departments, programming, and collection development. Space was designated for children so that programming, initially focused on children's storytime, could take place. In 1897, the Brooklyn Pratt Institute in New York opened a children's department.[7] I can't help but share this incredible observation: "'Such was the passion and wildness to see and enjoy these beautiful books,' the *Christian Advocate* noted, 'that the boys jumped in and out of the windows, slid down the stair rails, and made such an uproar that the Pratt people were alarmed.'"[8] This alarm saw Mary Wright Plummer hired, who was, "endowed with such patience and discretion and knowledge of the temperament of the children that she has become a guide to them in their reading."[9] Adding to the name-dropping here, Plummer hired an early twentieth-century pioneer in children's librarianship, Anne Carroll Moore, an educator and advocate for children; she was especially invested in promoting children's libraries.[10]

It was recognized in these early days that advocacy was needed on behalf of children and public libraries. In 1896, a Milwaukee librarian expounded on the importance of separate areas for children in the public library, noting that "The children's room should be airy and bright, contain a variety of plants, have open stacks, small yet comfortable chairs and tables, walls large enough for framed pictures, and bulletin boards to hang children's artwork."[11]

According to Elizabeth Fathauer and Mike Rogalla, looking back at the history of children's services at the Champaign Library in Illinois, they noted that fully eighteen years before the Chicago Public Library held its first children's program in 1899, the Champaign Library introduced a celebration around the autumn holidays for children in which University of Illinois library students collaborated with the public library by working with the librarians as well as loaning program materials, including Halloween posters; at that event, Miss Bennett spoke to children on a Saturday about Halloween customs, and library students rotated turns to further inform kids about Halloween. Thus was born the Saturday afternoon storytime in the Champaign Public Library.[12]

Noted by Fathauer and Rogalla, programming was established in 1899, and soon after, in the early 1900s, children were taught to care for books. Further, children's books had been separated from the adult collection and began to find space in the newly designated space for children's materials and instruction included admonitions in no way resembling children's presence in today's library. The Champaign Public Library organized the Library League of children, which included a kind of pledge that children be seen and not heard. Also reported in Fathauer and Rogalla's piece, Lillian Arnold and Marjorie Graves's note in their University of Illinois bachelor thesis that "'We, the undersigned members of the Library League, agree to do all in our power to assist the Librarian in keeping the books in good condition. We promise to remember that good books contain the living thoughts of the good and great men and women and are therefore entitled to respect.... When in the Library we will step softly and move quietly and try not to annoy other readers by any unnecessary noise or talking.... The motto was 'Clean hearts, clean hands, clean books.'"[13] Of course, librarians still want clean books and encourage clean hands while handling them as well as teaching children responsibility and respect for library materials, but there is typically no requirement to create a pledge as such.

According to Encyclopedia.com, these early establishments of children's services in public libraries resulted from progressive social reform movements of nineteenth-century librarians in both the United Kingdom and the United States that emphasized outreach and programming and the creation of children's collections. The goal was to function as a kind of support to school library efforts despite the public library retaining its focus on recreational reading. Public libraries eventually began to include areas for children's books, but it wasn't until the first library was constructed in the United States in 1895 that specific rooms for children became part of the library building; this design was featured regularly in libraries by the 1900s.[14] The first library to include a children's room, however, was the Boston Public Library.[15]

Early children's services in America focused primarily on school visits, book talks, storytelling, and other programs, and this foundational approach proved to influence librarians serving youth around the world.[16] To provide a wider perspective, not all nations approached children's services in this way; for example, India included children's sections in university libraries; in Iran, free-standing children's libraries, separate from other libraries, serve children and youth, and two libraries of note are the International Youth Library in Munich, and L'Heure Joyeuse in Paris.[17] Filioque L'Heure Joyeuse was founded by American philanthropic women immediately following WWI to honor the children of Belgium and France for having to endure the ravages of war; the library, still in existence today, opened its doors in 1924 and is officially known as a reference library for young people.[18] Among the many services offered, the library boasts three floors, includes 25,000 documents in its collection (books, CDs, DVDs), parenting books, and board games, among other things.[19] Finally, it's interesting to note that European librarians traveled to the United States to obtain special training.[20] Clearly, the United States was a forerunner in public library services.

As seen in the Champaign Public Library and alluded to earlier, storytimes were becoming a staple of burgeoning children's services in the United States. In 1896, story hours were introduced at the Pratt Institute by Anne Carroll Moore; Francis Jenkins Olcott established weekly storytimes in 1900 at the Carnegie Library of Pittsburgh, and in 1904, Caroline Burnite, in her role as assistant director, encouraged not only weekly storytimes but also established nursery tale story hours for the library's youngest patrons at their Broadway branch in 1906.[21]

For context, and to illustrate the development of more attention on children's services, between 1900 and 1901, the American Library Association (ALA) established the roundtable for children's librarians as well as a two-year training program for children's librarians that opened in Pittsburgh.[22]

Historical anecdotes offer a window into the past, and the following quotes shed light on the reception of storytime in its early days; you'll note that children's reflections and candor nearly always delight and often surprise. It was overheard in 1919 following a Saturday story hour at the Duluth Public Library in Minnesota about the librarian, "Ain't she some storyteller," and his friend chimed in with "I wish Saturday came every day."[23] Another anecdote from 1923 saw the Pittsburgh library offering an impromptu story hour on a summer afternoon. Seventy children sat in enrapt attention as the librarian read stories; the library noted that they provided around 3,000 story hours to 130,000 children that year.[24] Finally, every era sees new technology, and at least initially, people tend to approach these new apparatuses with concern and maybe even a little fear. Today, the ubiquitous iPhone causes worry for caregivers, but in the early 1920s, librarians worried about the radio as a means of drawing readers away from books; they mused, "thousands now sit back in comfortable chairs with their eyes closed listening to lectures, concerts and news broadcasts from general centers of entertainment,"[25] and this led to the reduction of some programming due to the radio's invention. Rather than being fearful of the radio, the invention and imagination of librarians saw libraries beginning radio programs and creating cross-continent contests involving the radio.[26] Along that same line, in 1954, the television was introduced, and libraries found themselves working hard to find new ways of attracting young patrons who had apparently abandoned books for television programs.[27] I fully admit to being one of those children, albeit a few years later! My after-school routine was to get off the bus, let myself into the apartment where my mother and I lived, and turn on the TV to watch *Gilligan's Island*—my absolute favorite show.

A POOR SHOWING OF EQUAL ACCESS TO ALL

In terms of equal access to public libraries for all races, the historical record is abysmal. Departing briefly from historical children's services, it's important to have a look at the public library, the ALA, and the Jim Crow South. Note that though libraries at this time claimed to be open to all, it was simply not the case; black Americans were barred from whites-only libraries.[28]

It wasn't until 1922, forty-six years after the ALA was formed in 1876, that Thomas Fountain Blue addressed the ALA Round Table on Work with Negroes. This was an unprecedented speech; Blue, the library director of two black branches of the library in Louisville, Kentucky, was the first black American to address an ALA conference session. From that address, the first library services field of study was implemented at the Hampton Institute in Virginia; here, education was available "to train librarians for the 'colored branches of city library systems.'"[29]

The following anecdote of Richard Wright, author of the 1940 novel *Native Son* and his autobiographical title *Black Boy* in 1945, shows his clever subversion of Jim Crow public library practices: "As a sixth grader in Jackson, Mississippi, he marveled at a *Chicago Defender* article describing 'Lake Michigan Negroes' who went to public libraries and took out any book they wanted."[30] This was certainly not the case at the Memphis Public Library, though black people could check out books from the library for white people for whom they worked. Wright ingeniously devised a plan to have a white man agree to allow him the use of his wife's library card. Wright then forged a note and included a derogatory word to ensure the note seemed authentically from a white person. With the note in hand, Wright explains that he nervously waited patiently at the circulation desk and took on a demeanor that he thought may not betray his education. When the white librarian finally helped Wright, she asked, "'What do you want, boy?' As though I did not possess the power of speech, I stepped forward and simply handed her the forged note, not parting my lips. 'What books by Mencken does she want?' she asked. 'I don't know, ma'am,' I said, avoiding her eyes . . . 'You're not using these books, are you?' she asked pointedly. 'Oh, no, ma'am. I can't read.'"[31]

Overt measures were taken to enforce Jim Crow laws in the South to ensure that libraries remained whites only, but in other regions of the country, enforcement of various laws worked to ensure that black people were denied access—public buildings, like schools and libraries, were "protected" by the 1896 Supreme Court *Plessy v. Ferguson* decision to ensure "separate but equal" was upheld.[32]

Noted in a case study of Atlanta from The Digital Library of America, activists, including prolific author W.E.B. DuBois, spoke out against discrimination in libraries, and though their protests did not effect change, Andrew Carnegie and other philanthropists were eventually inspired to build library branches for black people; the first was in Louisville, Kentucky, in 1905, and Atlanta followed in 1921. It wasn't until 1959 that the Atlanta-Fulton Public Library System desegregated. Indeed, progress for equal access to libraries across the nation was slow, and services were nonexistent for the better part of the early twentieth century.[33]

Library sit-ins happened! The 1960 Greensboro, North Carolina, sit-in is most often referenced in discussions around civil rights protests, but less known is the arrest of Ethel Sawyer in 1961; Sawyer and eight other members of the National Association for the Advancement of Colored People (NAACP) Youth Council staged a sit-in at the white-only library in Jackson, Mississippi.[34] Integration occurred in fits and starts at local levels in some areas around the United States, but three events occurred to begin the steps toward more equal access around the nation: first, the *Brown v. Board of Education* Supreme Court case, which overturned *Plessy*; second, the Civil Rights Act of 1964, and third, the Voting Rights Act of 1965.[35]

One way in which libraries made progress toward improving community relationships was in the development of the library's role into a more robust community service center. Barbara Clark of the Los Angeles Public Library was a key figure in transforming the library from being primarily book-centered to becoming a community center. Prior to 1968, Clark offered a broad spectrum of creative and fun children's programs that included youth watching television shows like *Sesame Street* and *The Electric Company* in the library and holding tricycle races and rock band performances in the library parking lot, among other things.[36]

Hispanic communities also saw the library becoming a community center. "At one Los Angeles County Public Library, a Mexican American artist painted a twenty-foot mural of a brown man bursting his bonds. Another, located in a neighborhood lacking a movie theater, hosted a monthly film night and puppet shows put on by barrio children."[37]

Pura Belpré is an important figure in public library history, and she has been commemorated with an American Library Association award, The Pura Belpré award, which "is presented to a Latino/Latina writer and illustrator whose work best portrays, affirms, and celebrates the Latino cultural experience in an outstanding work of literature for children and youth."[38] Belpré was a gifted storyteller. She grew up in Puerto Rico where her grandmother told her stories and whose unique characters Belpré often featured in her storytimes at the New York Public Library; she visited New York in 1920 to attend her sister's wedding, but she wanted to stay, having fallen in love with the city.[39] Belpré has the distinction of being the first New York City Puerto Rican librarian as well as having her beloved stories and puppets published as books, which include *Perez and Martina* (1932) and *Juan Bobo and the Queen's Necklace* (1962).[40]

While these librarians had a positive effect on their respective communities, many areas of the United States still saw challenges to integration at the public library. The process was slow, and while there were some advances, entrenched historical cultural norms often prevented equal access to library services. Certainly, libraries and librarians have adapted over the decades and continue to assess how they might ensure service to all.[41] For a rich and far more in-depth look at the history of public libraries, be sure to read Wiegand's work *Part of Our Lives: A People's History of the American Public Library*.

FOUNDING MOTHERS

To complete this very brief history of programming in libraries, I include the work of Betsy Hearne and Christine Jenkins, who researched the founders, what they call the foremothers' of library services to children. They drew interesting conclusions after careful reading of the founders' published works, referred to by Hearne and Jenkins as "sacred texts."[42] Among those texts were Anne Carroll Moore's 1920 *My Road to Childhood*, Frances Clarke Sayers' 1937 *Summoned by Books*, and Annis Duff's 1944 *Bequest of Wings*; these women inspired a generation of librarians in the 1950s and 1960s, reaching as far as Ruth Hill Viguers's 1964 *About Books, Children, and Librarians*.[43] Quoting one another heavily throughout their careers, their terminology referenced librarianship as an almost biblical calling and vocation. These foremothers focused primarily on reading and enriching the lives of children, understood the value of placing children first, and recognized the librarian as a key role model in a young person's life in what they considered an almost holy endeavor; this can be seen in the following statement: "The library boiled down to the individual who ran it. She was a reader with a mission to create more readers. Love and respect for literature and children had to center every program. The day belonged to the book and the child, cataloging and shelving be damned (or at least recognized as a lower order of ritual)."[44] I urge you to read the Hearne and Jenkins article, "Sacred Texts: What Our Foremothers Left Us in the Way of Psalms, Proverbs,

Precepts, and Practices," to comprehend how deeply these women influenced future generations.

Note that this is a very brief overview of the rich and varied history of library integration in the United States and is merely an appetizer to what is truly a full meal of historical information in libraries. Further exploration is encouraged as it is beyond the scope of this book to delve more deeply.

CHILDREN'S PROGRAMMING: DEFINITIONS AND VALUE

I'll start this section by looking back on my early days as a children's librarian, beginning, incredibly, as the Head of Youth Services. I think about how green I was as I worked toward providing a collection for the children of the town as well as incorporating programming that would be interesting and exciting; this was my first foray into library work ... ever. I drove myself to understand the community I served as an initial step, and from there, I explored programming that I thought would appeal to the youth of the community. Naturally, as a new librarian, I was excited and wanted to try *All. The. Programs!* Having recently retired from teaching middle school, I wanted to bring the excitement of reading to kids from the classroom to the library. I didn't realize it at the time, but my goal aligned with the focus of any public library: good programming connects kids with literacy and encourages a life-long desire for learning, which just makes good sense. In my enthusiasm to create new programs, I experienced both the joys of a packed house and the anxiety over complete flops. Regardless, I enjoyed the support of the library community and administration and felt confident in taking risks and being expansive in my thinking; I hope this book encourages you to do the same.

DEFINING CHILDREN'S PROGRAMMING: VALUE IN PUBLIC LIBRARIES

So, what is a library program? It may seem obvious—librarians create an activity connected in some way to books and literacy, and they advertise the event. Kids arrive (hopefully in droves) to participate. Done! While that may be the simplistic view of programming, considering elements of programming and what comprises a good program is our focus here.

The Wichita Public Library has created this helpful definition that is inclusive of all components and considerations of the library: "A program is defined as an event sponsored or co-sponsored by the library, having a presentation component and lasting 20 minutes or longer. A program can be a single event or a series of events, be a scheduled or a pop-up event, take place inside or outside of a library, or take place online. Programming furthers the mission, vision and values of the Wichita Public Library."[45] Following this foundational definition, Wichita Public outlines further details about programming: "Programming is a fundamental component of library service that: introduces attendees to library resources and materials; provides learning and entertainment opportunities to meet the informational, education and recreational needs of those attending the program; raises awareness and visibility of the library to the community; supports and responds to emerging community interests as well as established interest and demands; expands the Library's role as a cultural and community center; and/or extends outreach for underserved populations."[46]

The framework outlined in the Wichita Public Library's policy on programming is clearly stated, detailed, and provides staff with the necessary platform on which to build programs of interest to the community. Does your library have a programming policy? Are key components outlined in detail? If you find no such policy at your library, consider advocating for establishing one. If your library does have a policy, frequent review is important. I'll speak more about this in later chapters.

Adele Fasick and Leslie Edmonds Holt, in *Managing Children's Services in Libraries*, take a further step in outlining what programming for children should look like by including first, the development of reading skills and assistance in helping children access library materials; second, having a provision of enrichment (likely unconnected to reading skill development); and third, having the concept that programs may help to make the library more visible to the community—thus focusing on marketing as a program goal.[47] According to Fasick and Holt, the common denominator in all these goals is that "the librarian is the intermediary between the collection and the audience."[48] This is an interesting perspective, and I admit that I did not plan programs with the goal of making the library visible; that I may have inadvertently accomplished this was a bonus.

The important questions a librarian must ask about programming include whether the program is solely focused on the child; what the children of the community need; in what ways are child participants enriched; whether the program connects children with books and literacy; and does the program relate to the mission of the library? These were at the forefront when I began program planning. Beginning with these questions in mind, the outcome of library marketing falls into place, and it's my thought that further focus on marketing around programming doesn't need specific attention. In other words, I wouldn't hold a program that may or may not fit the needs of the community just to appear flashy; focus on the community and you'll naturally market the library.

To begin thinking about programming, here are some guidelines to get you started. First, get to know your community. Read the census, and chat with colleagues and community members to understand the demographics of your town, county, city, or neighborhood. Now consider the diversity of your population. If you find yourself in an area lacking in diverse populations, think about ways you might incorporate cultures other than the predominant culture into your programming; how might you expand and widen your young patrons' worldview? Another consideration is to look at your own interests; I found that my passion for beading bracelets, baking cupcakes, knitting, studying herbs and plants, all things Harry Potter, cycling, and even for Shakespeare found its way into my program concepts. Young people pick up on your vibe, so if you're really into something, they'll notice it and get excited, too. More on these details later, but I want to mention here that even the books you read and share for storytime should be titles you love.

EXEMPLARY CHILDREN'S PROGRAMMING: AN INITIATIVE

I can't think of a better framework for successful programming that gets to the heart of what comprises outstanding programming than the Association for Library Service to Children's (ALSC) Curiosity Creates grant. In 2015, the Walt Disney Company funded the initiative for seventy-nine public libraries at up to $7,500 each "to promote and develop creativity skills in children ages 6 to 14, focusing on one or more of the seven critical components of creativity."[49] Based upon research from the Bay Area Discovery Museum white paper "Inspiring a Generation to Create: Critical Components of Creativity in Children," authors Helen Hadini and Garret Jaegar outlined components critical to creativity that informed the project.[50]

The seven components outlined in the project were:

1. Imagination and Originality: Imagine and explore original ideas
2. Flexibility: Maintain openness to unique and novel experiences
3. Decision Making: Make thoughtful choices that support creative efforts
4. Communication and Self-Expression: Communicate ideas and true self with confidence
5. Motivation: Demonstrate internal motivation to achieve a meaningful goal
6. Collaboration: Develop social skills that foster teamwork
7. Action and Movement: Boost creative potential through physical activity

Further keys to success in defining programming for children are outlined in the ALSC's *Competencies for Librarians Serving Children in Libraries*, which lists nine skills; each of the seven of the nine skills listed here deepens an understanding of what programming is and what exemplary programming includes; the two additional skills not listed include addressing the needs of caregivers and all who work with caregivers and providing programming to all patrons in formats that work for them.[51] The remaining seven skills are:

1. Designs, promotes, presents, and evaluates a variety of diverse programs for children, with consideration of equity, diversity, and inclusion; principles of child development; and the needs, interests, and goals of all children, their caregivers, and educators in the community.

2. Acknowledges the importance of physical space to engage and foster learning and establishes appropriate environments for programs that respond to developmental needs and abilities of children and families.
3. Acknowledges the importance of the caregiver-child bond to early learning and establishes appropriate and effective environments for programs that respond to the social and emotional needs of children and create opportunities for families to engage in programming together.
4. Integrates technology in program design and delivery appropriate for children and families.
5. Integrates literacy-development techniques in program design and delivery, engaging and empowering caregivers in a culturally aware way.
6. Designs programs that foster a variety of literacies and learning methods including, but not limited to, pre-literacy, early literacy, family literacy, media literacy, technology literacy, computational thinking, STEM, and maker-centered learning.
7. Identifies, engages, and supports colleagues, coworkers, and community members from diverse backgrounds to contribute ideas and skills for programs and presentations.[52]

From this comprehensive list, our definition, along with the key elements of library programming for children, is more fully fleshed out.

Summarizing this section, put simply, children's programming can be defined as an event held in the library or sponsored by the library that invites children to participate in an activity that in some way connects them to the library collection and literacy or provides enrichment in some way. Future chapters will explore the many varieties of programs that support this definition.

Now that we've established a solid programming definition, it's important to examine the educational development of children and how the library might enhance this formative time in a child's life.

THE VALUE OF EARLY LITERACY AND MULTILITERACY LEARNING: A FOUNDATION OF CHILDHOOD DEVELOPMENT

EARLY LITERACY

The study of childhood development is a vast and complicated field. Comprehending how children develop and what impact early literacy has on that development is key to offering exemplary library programs that serve this population. As with the history of children's services, this section is meant to provide fundamental concepts only; I encourage you to pursue further study in this area.

According to the Children's Medical Centre, the five stages of childhood development are (1) newborn—birth to three months; (2) infant—three age groups mark this stage: infants three to six months, infants six to nine months, and infants nine to twelve months; (3) toddler—one to three years; (4) preschooler—three to five years; and (5) school-age—six to seventeen years. Further details of the milestones and characteristics in each of these age groups are explained and can be easily found online.[53] For the purposes of this discussion, early literacy includes the education of children from birth to kindergarten.

Early literacy prepares the child for learning to read and write; it is not educating children on how to read. The ALA defines early literacy in this way: "Early literacy (reading and writing) does not mean early reading instruction or teaching babies to read; it is the natural development of skills through the enjoyment of books, the importance of positive interactions between babies and parents, and the critical role of literacy-rich experiences."[54] The Johnson County Library succinctly describes early literacy as "what children know about reading and writing before they actually learn to read and write. It is not teaching reading, drilling or using flashcards. Instead, it is laying the foundation . . . [for children to have] the necessary skills when they are developmentally ready to read."[55] These simple definitions serve the library well and help the librarian to focus on the joys of getting children and their caregivers excited about reading and other literacy-related activities. Along with the librarian's role, the caregivers' partnership in early literacy is a key to children's long-term success and lifelong literacy. In a study of three- to five-year-olds who were read to more than three times per week, "children were two times more likely to recognize all their letters, two times more likely to have word-sight recognition, and two times more likely to understand words in context."[56]

When looking at statistics around early literacy, a phenomenon known as the "Matthew Effect" comes into play. This concept is derived from the biblical passage that states that to those who have, more will be given, and to those who have not, even what little they have will be taken away; note that I'm paraphrasing here. As an explanation, typically, when children are provided with resources and, in this case, early literacy opportunities, they have a future forged from those early opportunities and meet with success that impacts many areas of their lives. Statistics indicate that for those who do not have early literacy opportunities, their progression is markedly inhibited and, in fact, do much more poorly. Libraries can potentially bridge a gap in early literacy development to provide early literacy opportunities.[57]

To understand a bit more about early literacy in relation to the library, a closer look at storytime and other programming best practices is in order. Perhaps the best baseline information about early literacy and its relationship to the library can be found in the Every Child Ready to Read (ECRR) initiative. The initiative itself included a seismic shift from focusing solely on the child to including caregivers in the library's efforts to increase early literacy; the focus on this initiative was to educate caregivers in what would become the five practices noted below. Grover Whitehurst and Christopher Lonigan developed the early literacy model that outlined six literacy skills as part of ECRR: (1) print awareness, (2) letter knowledge, (3) phonetical awareness, (4) vocabulary, (5) narrative skills, and (6) print motivation.[58] Later, these six skills morphed into five practices (singing, talking, reading, writing, and playing) and six literacy components (oral language, vocabulary, background knowledge, print conventions/awareness, letter knowledge, and phonetical awareness) in ECRR.[59]

Among the best resources for information on the ECRR initiative, some can be found at Saraj Ghoting's website earlylit.net; here, the librarian is provided with multiple tools to not only hold early literacy storytimes that include the five practices but also multiple methods of engaging caregivers in the important work of partnering in their child's early literacy—a partnership that is a lifelong endeavor and places the vital role of the caregiver in this partnership front and center. Library storytimes no longer see the caregiver as an observer, but rather, caregivers are encouraged to sing, dance, play, and participate fully in the early literacy storytime. Why? This fostering of caregiver education and a family-centric approach helps caregivers understand they are the most important people in a child's life and, as also mentioned in *Every Child Ready to Read Depends on Libraries Preparing Parents for Lifelong Involvement in Literacy*, "Through this practice, parents become confident in their ability to teach and encourage their children and children, in turn, begin seeing their parents as teachers and partners in their development."[60]

Including the five practices as well as fostering caregiver participation in storytimes by librarians has been done in some format from even the earliest offerings of storytime. It's long been thought that storytimes benefit children and their emerging literacy. A two-year comprehensive study of the impact of library storytimes and early literacy was conducted and reported on in 2017, and it was concluded that unmistakable evidence points to a direct correlation. Campana et al. conducted the first year of their study in Washington State to include the observation of approximately 1,440 children in forty libraries, viewing a total of 120 storytimes. Results overwhelmingly demonstrated "a positive correlation between the storytime provider's early literacy program content and the children's early literacy behaviors."[61] Tools used in this study to compile and evaluate data proved to be useful to a library's evaluation of early literacy outcomes in the public library storytimes.[62]

Early literacy concepts are primarily shown here through the lens of storytime, though they exist in other formats in the library as well. Understanding the workings of early literacy and how the librarian, especially those trained beyond their MLIS in further childhood development, can positively impact the lifelong learning and literacy of children when they engage caregivers and empower them to partner in their child's literacy.

Another element important in literacy development is dialogic reading, defined in the bulleted section that follows, and though this is typically considered a caregiver's responsibility, a librarian's awareness of dialogic reading relates to storytime effectiveness by engaging the young patrons in attendance. Often, the librarian or caregiver reads a story to a child and the child is an inactive listener; dialogic reading helps to engage the child in the story by asking them questions and encouraging participation. Having a participatory role at an early age helps establish a foundation on which to build lifelong literacy, launching a child far beyond their peers. According to Grover Whitehurst of *Reading Rockets*, dialogic reading involves four elements in the PEER sequence that:

1. Prompts the child to say something about the book;
2. Evaluates the child's response;
3. Expands the child's response by rephrasing and adding information to it; and
4. Repeats the prompt to make sure the child has learned from the expansion.[63]

Whitehurst further explains this sequence by providing the following example: "Imagine that the caregiver and the child are looking at the page of a book that has a picture of a fire engine on it. The parent says, 'What is this?' (the prompt) while pointing to the fire truck. The child says, 'truck,' and the parent follows with 'That's right (the evaluation); it's a red fire truck (the expansion); can you say fire truck?' (the repetition)."[64] In addition to engaging the storytime attendees, having children in the group who are more comfortable engaging will provide an example for those less inclined to speak out. Using a call-and-response technique based on the PEER sequencing not only helps advance literacy but also validates young people and lets them know they are part of the story.

These are but a few elements around the concept of early literacy; more will be explored in detail in subsequent chapters, especially related to storytime. The selection is intended to provide a foundational understanding of early literacy in the context of librarianship. Multiliteracy is linked to early literacy, and I'll point out those connections in the next section.

MULTILITERACY

The origin of this newer term is interesting. The New London Group, a group of ten international scholars who met in New London, New Hampshire, coined the term "multiliteracies" in the 1990s when they sought to examine classroom teaching and improve upon and update methodologies and pedagogy.[65] Briefly, pedagogy can be described as how teachers teach—a simplistic definition that works for now. With the digital age upon us, this innovative approach has offered an excellent framework to help the literacy development of children and to understand the shifting field of communication in our technologically advancing world.

The term refers to the multiple ways that humans communicate and offers five modes of multiliteracy. Explained in detail, Lynn Baker sheds light on each of these modes. The five modes are (1) Visual Literacy, (2) Textual Literacy, (3) Social Literacy, (4) Digital Media Literacy, and (5) Multisensory Literacy.[66] Examining these modes provides insight for the children's librarian, but note that this information is descriptive of the typically developing child; exploration of serving children with disabilities is forthcoming in its own chapter.

Visual literacy is a skill that is situated at the center of the four other modes as elements of this method of communication are most essential and overlap with the four other areas. Essentially, visual literacy is intricately connected to social literacy and enables the child to "visually find, interpret, and use information that is being communicated, whether through text, pictures, or symbols."[67] Social cues come into play when children are required to interpret body language and facial expressions—if these skills are not present, then the child will struggle to interact socially.

Baker reminds readers that textual literacy, the second mode of multiliteracies, is what most people think of when the term *literacy* is used. This makes sense as this literacy is related to the reading and comprehending of the printed word.[68]

Social literacy, the third mode, overlaps visual literacy, as mentioned earlier, but it also finds a connection to textual literacy. Remember our discussion of dialogic reading? Social literacy is tied to this form of early literacy approach for the librarian. Here, social interactions are directly connected to the reading of text when children are challenged to connect to the text through open-ended questions, prediction, and other engagement.[69]

A primary focus for the previously mentioned New London Group is the emergence of technology and the requirements necessary to communicate effectively through various technological methods. Similarly, digital media literacy, according to Baker, "encompasses a variety of communication methods that are associated with technology use. . . . [it] includes accessing and creating information that is delivered through electronic means, as well as the ability to communicate effectively through e-mail, social media, and other technology-based platforms."[70] Keeping in mind that technology is advancing rapidly, it's important for the librarian to be digitally savvy by seeking out and exploring new technologies.

Finally, Baker states that multisensory literacy "refers to all the ways in which a child interacts with information and communication through hands-on, active manipulation."[71] Including opportunities for play and interactive experiences in programming will address this most important mode of literacy for youth. Why? Play and multisensory literacy are critical to children's development as they involve "all the child's senses that are appropriate to a given activity (seeing, hearing, touching, smelling, and moving) and helps the child's brain develop tactile, auditory, and visual memories, which, in turn, helps the child retain learned information."[72] I admit to not having had this terminology as a young librarian, but as seen in other areas of programming, the intuitive inclusion of craft time following storytime and other hands-on activities served this final mode of multiliteracy.

While this is a small sampling of foundational elements for the children's librarian, a good understanding of these concepts will lead to further research and reading and will ultimately inform the practice of programming for children with the knowledge of how that population learns and what literacy development will look like.

DEVELOPMENT AND VALUE OF LIFELONG LEARNERS

As with other sections in this chapter, I'll begin with a definition of lifelong learners. Sounds like a silly decision, maybe? It's almost obvious that a person described as a lifelong learner will, well, be someone who's a learner for his, her, or their lives. Right? The best place to start, then, is to work through the difference between a lifelong learner and lifelong learning. It appears, according to Sherry Crow, that there is some debate over details in the definition, but for the purposes of this writing, I'll go with Crow's description of lifelong learners as "people who display an attitude and ability that prompts them to learn across their lifespans."[73] Crow continues to outline a solid series of attributes that define a lifelong learner, but key to them all is the need for personal motivation—an element required for success in the area of lifelong learning.[74] This motivation, again, according to Crow's research, is present despite the grind of daily life; interest in subjects reaches beyond the mundane, and the lifelong learner may become so enrapt in learning in a new field or area that they're able to sustain interest in their focus despite personal needs, such as hunger or sleep.[75]

I've established something of a working definition, but how does that relate to the librarian and children's programming in the public library? As guidance, let's look at the library I'm affiliated with in Rye, New Hampshire. Looking at the Rye Public Library's (RPL) Mission Statement, it reads, "The Rye Public Library will be a friendly and inviting place providing unrestricted access to an array of materials, programs, and technologies that inform, educate, and entertain. We will promote the value of reading and encourage the quest for knowledge and experience to enrich lifelong learning, discovery, and creativity. The Library will be a mine of good and a fountain of help in the guiding spirit of our original benefactor, Mary Tuck Rand."[76] There is something of a clue here in that the RPL may encourage lifelong learning through its provision of access to materials, programs, and technologies and through its promotion of reading and seeking out knowledge and experience. Sounds good, right? Consider the notion put forth by the International Federation of Library Associations and Institutions (IFLA) that by providing worldwide access to information, even in a small library, the library is, in fact, promoting lifelong learning. The IFLA report on public libraries and lifelong learning goes on to mention that this basis of information access is critical, yet it's incumbent upon the librarian to provide assistance to patrons, and therefore, the librarian must be current on forms of technology that connect even the smallest library to a worldwide network of information.[77]

When I reflect on the creation of lifelong learners in the public library, I can understand and appreciate the offerings mentioned earlier, but thinking on a more personal note, the nature of the librarian must be considered. A librarian who exudes enthusiasm and offers help to all patrons, even those patrons who may be reluctant to ask for help, will assist in the lifelong learning process. Access to information is wonderful, but the help afforded by a librarian is invaluable and will help a motivated, or even an unmotivated, patron seek information and understand they have a partner in their journey to knowledge and, hopefully, to lifelong learning.

Historical anecdotes provide a window into past library services for children, as I mentioned, and as the profession developed, refinements were made to accommodate youth and their library needs. This very brief and selective inclusion of the library's history is obviously quite limited, but it should shed a little light on the library of the past, which should be helpful in informing the library of today. Also in this chapter, I've established some elements of programming and early literacy that will form the foundation for future chapters.

REVIEW QUESTIONS

1. After reading the brief history of children's services in libraries, did you find any surprises? Write a paragraph on your reflection.
2. Explore further in the areas of equity, diversity, inclusion, and belonging; examine more deeply the historical issues and compare them to today's library. What has changed? What hasn't?
3. Outline best practices for early literacy in storytimes.
4. Define multiliteracy and determine the connection between this concept and the library's role in early education.
5. What are the foundational elements of learning; research further to determine a more in-depth understanding. Why is this important to the librarian?
6. What is the partnership role that the librarian has with caregivers in early literacy efforts?
7. Explain dialogic reading and how this relates to storytime.

NOTES

1. Nicholas Rizzo, "State of US Public Libraries—More Popular & Digital Than Ever," accessed February 17, 2022, https://wordsrated.com/state-of-us-public-libraries/.

2. Ibid.
3. Kathryn Sickhur, Lee Rainie, and Kristen Purcell, "Part 5: Parents, Children, and Libraries," accessed December 4, 2022, https://www.pewresearch.org/internet/2013/05/01/part-5-parents-children-and-libraries/.
4. Pew Research Center, "Library Services in the Digital Age," accessed December 4, 2022, https://www.pewresearch.org/internet/2013/01/22/part-4-what-people-want-from-their-libraries/.
5. Virginia Walter, *Children and Libraries: Getting it Right* (Chicago: American Library Association, 2000), 1.
6. Ibid.; Rizzo, "State of US Public Libraries."
7. Wayne A. Wiegand, *Part of Our Lives: A People's History of the American Public Library* (Oxford: University Press, 2015), 83.
8. Ibid.
9. Ibid.
10. Ibid.
11. Ibid.
12. Elizabeth Fathauer and Mike Rogalla, "Celebrating a Century of Serice [sic] to Children: A History of Children's Services at the Champaign Public Library, 1899–1999," accessed February 3, 2024, https://www.lib.niu.edu/2000/il000109.html.
13. Ibid.
14. Encyclopedia.com, "Children's Libraries," accessed December 4, 2022, https://www.encyclopedia.com/children/encyclopedias-almanacs-transcripts-and-maps/childrens-libraries.
15. Boston Public Library, "About the BPL," accessed December 22, 2022, https://www.bpl.org/about-the-bpl/.
16. Encyclopedia.com, "Children's Libraries."
17. Ibid.
18. Mary Niles Maack. "L'Heure Joyeuse, the First Children's Library in France: Its Contribution to a New Paradigm for Public Libraries." *The Library Quarterly: Information, Community, Policy* 63, no. 3 (1993): 257–81. http://www.jstor.org/stable/4308835.
19. Ibid.
20. Ibid.
21. *American Library Association*, "History of Preschool Storytimes," accessed December 4, 2022, https://www.ala.org/tools/history-preschool-storytimes.
22. Ibid.
23. Wiegand, *Part of Our Lives*, 131.
24. Ibid., 131.
25. Ibid., 132–33.
26. Ibid., 132–33.
27. Fathauer and Rogalla, "Celebrating a Century of Serice [sic] to Children."
28. Wiegand, *Part of Our Lives*, 112.
29. Ibid., 112.
30. Ibid., 113.
31. Ibid., 113–14.
32. Digital Public Library of America. "A History of US Libraries," accessed December 5, 2022, https://dp.la/exhibitions/history-us-public-libraries/segregated-libraries.
33. Ibid.

34. Ibid.
35. Ibid.
36. Wiegand, *Part of Our Lives*, 202.
37. Ibid., 202.
38. Association for Library Services to Children, "Pura Belpré Award," accessed February 3, 2024, https://www.ala.org/alsc/awardsgrants/bookmedia/belpre.
39. New York Public Library Staff, "Pura Belpré: Library Storyteller," accessed February 3, 2024, https://www.nypl.org/blog/2020/11/12/pura-belpre-library-storyteller.
40. Ibid.
41. Wiegand, *Part of Our Lives*, 202.
42. Betsy Hearne and Christine Jenkins, "Sacred Texts: What Our Foremothers Left Us in the Way of Psalms, Proverbs, Precepts, and Practices," *The Horn Book Magazine*, September 1999, 536.
43. Ibid.
44. Ibid.
45. Wichita Public Library, "Definition of a program," accessed December 5, 2022, https://www.wichitalibrary.org/library-programming#:~:text=A%20program%20is%20defined%20as,library%2C%20or%20take%20place%20online.
46. Ibid.
47. Adele M. Fasick and Leslie Edmonds Holt, *Managing Children's Services in Libraries*, 4th ed. (Santa Barbara, CA: Libraries Unlimited), 123.
48. Ibid.
49. Paula Holmes, "*ALSC Curiosity creates: Innovative library programming for children*," accessed December 4, 2022, https://www.ala.org/alsc/sites/ala.org.alsc/files/content/awardsgrants/minigrants/ALSC_Curiosity_Creates_Best_Practices_Final.pdf.
50. Ibid.
51. American Library Association—ALSC, "*Competencies for Librarians Serving Children in Libraries*," accessed December 9, 2022, https://www.ala.org/alsc/edcareeers/alsccorecomps.
52. Ibid.
53. Children's Medical Center, "The 5 stages of early childhood development," accessed December 12, 2022, https://www.npcmc.com/2022/07/08/the-5-stages-of-early-childhood-development/.
54. American Library Association, "Early Literacy: What We Know About Early Literacy," accessed December 12, 2022, https://www.ala.org/united/products_services/booksforbabies/earlyliteracy.
55. Johnson County Library, "*Early literacy*," accessed December 10, 2022, https://www.pageafterpage.org/early-literacy#:~:text=What%20is%20Early%20Literacy%3F,are%20developmentally%20ready%20to%20read.
56. American Library Association, "Early Literacy."
57. UWA Online, "Overcoming the Matthew Effect in Early Education," accessed December 22, 2022, https://online.uwa.edu/news/matthew-effect/#:~:text=Enter%20the%20Matthew%20Effect.,who%20begin%20poorly%20do%20worse.
58. Institute of Museum and Library Service, "Every Child Ready to Read Depends on Libraries Preparing Parents for Lifelong Involvement in Literacy," accessed December

12, 2022, https://www.imls.gov/grant-spotlights/every-child-ready-read-depends-libraries-preparing-parents-lifelong-involvement.
59. Kathleen Campana, J. Elizabeth Mills, Janet L. Capps, Eliza T. Dresang, Allyson Carlyle, Cheryl A. Metoyer, Ivette Bayo Urban, et al., "Early Literacy in Library Storytimes: A Study of Measures of Effectiveness," *Library Quarterly* 86, no. 4, (2016): 369-88.
60. Institute of Museum and Library Service, "Every Child Ready to Read."
61. Campana et al., "Early Literacy in Library Storytimes."
62. Ibid.
63. Grover J. (Russ) Whitehurst, "Reading Rockets, Dialogic reading: An effective way to read aloud with young children," accessed December 13, 2022, https://www.readingrockets.org/article/dialogic-reading-effective-way-read-aloud-young-children.
64. Ibid.
65. IGI Global, "What is New London Group," accessed December 13, 2022, https://www.igi-global.com/dictionary/new-london-group/85010#:~:text=1.,the%20term%20multiliteracies%20in%201994.
66. R. Lynn Baker, *Creating Literacy-based Programs for Children: Lesson Plans and Printable Resources for K-5* (Chicago: ALA Editions, 2017), 13-18.
67. Ibid., 14.
68. Ibid., 15.
69. Ibid., 15
70. Ibid., 17.
71. Ibid., 17.
72. Ibid., 17-18.
73. Sherry R. Crow, "What Motivates a Lifelong Learner?" *School Libraries Worldwide* 12, no. 1: 22-34. https://search-ebscohost-com.libaccess.sjlibrary.org/login.aspx?direct=true&db=eft&AN=21132962&site=ehost-live&scope=site.
74. Ibid., 23.
75. Ibid., 24.
76. Board of Trustees, Rye Public Library, "Library mission and vision statements," accessed December 13, 2022, https://ryepubliclibrary.org/library-mission-statements/.
77. B. M. Häggström, ed., "The role of public libraries in lifelong learning: Final report of the IFLA project under the section for public libraries," accessed December 13, 2022, https://www.ifla.org/g/public-libraries/the-role-of-public-libraries-in-lifelong-learning-a-project-under-the-section-of-public-libraries-ifla/.

2

Program Evaluation

PLANNING FOR DESIRED RESULTS

You may be surprised to learn that prior to my start as a very green Head of Youth Services in the public library, I rarely frequented libraries as a patron unless on a school visit as a young student. Despite being untrained in the ways of libraries, when I undertook the role of Head of Youth Services, I called on my instincts to guide me as I prepared programming for youth ages from birth to age eighteen. I imagine many new and unschooled librarians might begin by conducting online searches of what libraries near and far are doing in the way of children's programming. Fortunately for me, my former career as a middle school teacher provided a decent baseline of experience.

Whether I consciously evaluated my methods and programming or not, I utilized a trial-and-error method, trying all sorts of programming—nearly anything and everything, and I hoped something would stick. I watched as programs were successful and well-attended and others that had few or, on the rare occasion, no attendees. Over time, I began to learn what was popular with the youth in my town, and I figured out, perhaps the hard way, what they were and weren't interested in doing for library programming.

Over the years, I experienced success in program offerings, which culminated in competency; this was based on a project I completed in my library school program. To avoid the pitfalls of trial and error I experienced, you might consider the following options of expert outcome-based planning and evaluation methods. From reporting on Project Outcome to the methodology of Melissa Gross, Cindy Mediavilla, and Virgina A. Walter in *5 Steps of Outcome-Based Planning & Evaluation*, I'll summarize these important approaches in this chapter.

I have found that the best resources when planning and implementing programs begin with the library's mission, vision, and value statements, which are all inherently present in the library's strategic plan. I'll examine the model of the library where I work, the Rye Public Library (RPL) in New Hampshire, measured against each of these elements. To set the stage, consider the simple descriptions provided by this Michael Allison quote: "A mission statement is a statement of purpose, a vision statement is a vivid image of the future you seek to create, and a value statement outlines your organization's guiding concepts and beliefs."[1] These elements may seem similar, but there are important nuanced differences that make each unique.

When planning and implementing children's programming, it is these foundational elements that ultimately guide the librarian in evaluating whether the library's goals have been met. Consider this simple process: Prior to developing a program, I conducted a self-check and examined the goal of a program, comparing it to and ensuring alignment with foundational library goals. Only on rare occasions did I have to abandon a programming concept due to its lack of goal alignment; nearly all library programming fundamentally seeks to "better" a person through literature, life skills, or crafting projects, as examples. Now I'll explore the mission, vision, and value statements.

THE LIBRARY'S MISSION STATEMENT

A library mission statement should be succinct and include answers to these questions, as noted by Webjunction: What does the library do? Who does the library serve? How does the library serve those patrons?[2] Here's the RPL Mission Statement to see if it holds up to this standard:

> The Rye Public Library will be a friendly and inviting place providing unrestricted access to an array of materials, programs, and technologies that inform, educate, and entertain. We will promote the value of reading and encourage the quest for knowledge and experience to enrich lifelong learning, discovery, and creativity. The Library will be a mine of good and a fountain of help in the guiding spirit of our original benefactor, Mary Tuck Rand.[3]

To answer our question, let's first consider this question: What does the library do? The RPL

1. Provides a friendly and inviting space;
2. Provides unrestricted access to materials, programs, and technologies;
3. Promotes the value of reading;
4. Encourages the quest for knowledge and experience to enrich lifelong learning, discovery, and creativity;
5. Is a mine of good; and
6. Is a fountain of help.

You'll notice that the first four stated missions are clear and provide an answer to what the library does. The final two clearly harken back to the benefactor of the library, Mary Tuck Rand, and they might fit better in a value statement as they really outline guiding concepts and beliefs. In fact, the RPL does not currently include a value statement; if they did, this might well be part of it.

In terms of youth programming, the youth librarians at RPL can easily find a foundation upon which to build their children's and teen programming. First, each program should be rooted in providing a friendly and inviting space for each program; young patrons should have unrestricted access to the programs being offered, and the programs should encourage a love of reading and/or a quest for knowledge and experience to enrich a young patron's learning, discovery, and creativity. Therefore, the youth librarian has a solid foundation upon which programming can be built.

THE LIBRARY'S VISION STATEMENT

Looking more closely at Allison's quote about a vision statement being "a vivid image of the future you seek to create,"[4] here are more details, and again, I'll measure vision statement qualities against the RPL version. Asana, a web and mobile "work management" platform, further expounds on the vividness required in a vision statement by including these four additional qualities: "a great vision statement should be ambitious, feasible, broad, and strategic."[5] These elements align well with the library despite the usage by Asana for a business-focused vision statement. Let's look at what the RPL developed and how it measures up:

> The vision of the Rye Public Library is to be the cultural heart of Rye by facilitating the free flow of ideas and information for all members of our community.[6]

Is this statement ambitious? I think so, but the town is small, and the library provides materials and programming to better the lives of those who are patrons. Because of this, and that there isn't competition on that front, I believe the library has met that lofty goal. Is the statement feasible? Indeed—it is perfectly within the realm of possibility that the library acts as a place in which ideas and information for all members of the community are available. Is the statement broad? Does it include all the library's goals under this wide-ranging umbrella? Again, it seems to: The library seeks to provide information and promote thinking about all manner of ideas to members of the town, so yes, this vision statement does include the library's goals. Finally, is the vision statement strategic? Does it describe an ideal future relevant to the library's goals or brand? Indeed it does—the ideal presented here aligns with the notion of including all members of the community and has determined its focus as becoming the cultural heart of the community that invites users to participate in a free flow of ideas and information. Overall, by these standards, RPL has done a good job with its statements; I encourage you to explore your own library to determine how it measures up.

THE LIBRARY'S STRATEGIC PLAN

Strategic planning is a multi-layered process that is complex; for our purposes, we'll be looking at a foundational structure of strategic planning as we continue to provide the groundwork for evaluative measures when planning for youth programming. From my experience, a strategic plan is defined as library administration, staff, and the community coming together to formulate a library's vision and goals for a defined period, which is typically five years. The Rye Public Library engaged in its first documented and widely distributed strategic planning effort dating from 2012–2015, beginning with a modest three-year focus; the subsequent planning period was 2018–2023, a five-year plan. Looking at these strategic plans, a focus on the community was a key element. Vision and mission statements were included in the final strategic planning document, and of course, goals and objectives were carefully developed around those statements.

Categories of goals and objectives shed light on programming and include community engagement, technology evaluation and planning, communication methods, facility standards, funding capacity, and outcomes measurement.[7] For the purposes of this chapter, the measurement appears to be inclusive, but there is not yet any mention of including qualitative data as a facet of outcome measurements.

In the updated and more recent strategic plan is the inclusion of a story—something that brought the community together and connected the readers; the 2018–2023 plan began with a lovely commemoration of a recently deceased and beloved staff member, Tricia Quinn, and included a stained-glass piece that incorporated sea glass Tricia had collected on the beach into the design along with a beautiful white heron—Tricia's favorite bird. My spouse Sylvia conceived of the idea and design of the project; community members met to adhere copper foil to pieces of glass while reminiscing about Tricia and healing together. It was lovely. The stained-glass piece with satellite stained-glass stars hangs in the bay window of the library's adult department. It's a colorful commemoration of Tricia, who was beloved by the community and staff. Highlighting the community participation in this project reminded strategic plan readers of Tricia's contributions to the community through her library work as well as unifying community members in her life and now through this beautiful project.

I'd like to share an anecdote that illustrates the importance of story and how stories can create personal connections. While developing plans for a planned library renovation and expansion project, the fundraiser we hired required the library to provide stories to connect people with the library. I remember being struck by and really loving the concept of helping the people in the town, whether library users or not, to realize the value the library held for so many people. We collected those stories, and despite the pandemic's thwarting of the project temporarily, I believe those stories will ultimately help the community realize the library's value.

Back to those statements, to be clear and for our purposes, the library's vision and mission statements and its strategic plan help establish goals and objectives that inform the library's program planning as well as provide the youth librarian with fundamental elements for program evaluation.

Now that we have the basis for our evaluation, determining how programs are measured is the next area to examine. To start, I'll have a look at how programs are measured traditionally, and I'll showcase two areas that provide exemplary program assessment, and it's not simply a reporting of numbers!

QUALITATIVE AND QUANTITATIVE MEASUREMENTS: REPORTING IN PUBLIC LIBRARIES

If your library is like most, you track numbers: how many participants in your programs, how many programs per month, how much of the budget was spent on your programs, and so on. Quantitative program measurement is all about numbers, yet, there is also much to be learned from qualitative reporting.

For clarity, these two terms are defined in the following way: "Quantitative data is numbers-based, countable, or measurable. Qualitative data is interpretation-based, descriptive, and relating to language."[8] To that definition, this further clarification may be helpful: "Quantitative data tells us how many, how much, or how often in calculations. Qualitative data can help us to understand why, how, or what happened behind certain behaviors."[9]

Reporting of public library usage statistics has not, in many states, realized the benefit and importance of qualitative reporting. It's not enough, as I've mentioned, to measure outcomes by the number of people present; what's needed is a measurement of any changes that may have occurred in a patron after attending a program. What has the patron learned? Did they grow? What benefit has been derived from attendance at the library program? I'll be looking at some practical methods of measurement, but before getting to that, let's see what is required from the public library in terms of annual reporting. Here again, I'm including the Rye Public Library and, subsequently, the State Library of New Hampshire to examine reporting requirements.

Statistics for 2021 required the following reporting components related to programs for children; the numbers in parentheses are the reported 2021 totals:

- *Reference Transactions Children's Programs On Site (include SRP)* (336,461)
- *Total Children's Programs* (this includes offsite, in-person, and virtual programs) (14,451)

- *Total Children's Program Attendance* (include SRP) (this includes offsite, in-person, and virtual program attendance) (118,768)
- *Attendance of Summer Reading Programs for Children* (54,032)[10]

From these numbers, it's clear that plenty of children's programs are being offered and kids are attending them—the numbers here tell that story. But is there a disservice in not knowing how these programs may have impacted the lives of the young patrons who came to the public library? According to Pia Gahagan and Philip Calvert, it is. Published in 2020, the article "Evaluating a Public Library Makerspace" reports on a public library's makerspace to determine methods employed to evaluate outcomes. The article outlines traditional measurement and reporting in public libraries as having focused on collection data and door counts; these numbers, it was thought, helped bolster library funding.[11] With a decline in circulation numbers in 2017, it was clear that this measurement method could not determine how patrons attending library programs have seen learning or improvement in their lives, and that any qualitative information derived from this quantitative measurement is inferred, following that with, "What is required is a greater understanding of the benefits libraries bring to the communities that serve them, and for that new measures are needed."[12] The study concluded that while some measures are being taken to gather qualitative data from programs, the process itself is in need of improvement. Specifically, the implications of the study concluded, "staff involved in running makerspaces may develop a formal approach to gathering outcomes data to use in combination with traditional quantitative data currently collected. A second implication is that staff may begin to take a more planned approach to developing programmes [sic] and services, ensuring assessment occurs regularly against well-articulated objectives aligned to wider organizational goals."[13] From this, it's clear that evaluative measures need to be employed to accurately depict true measurement of programming at a deeper and more meaningful level.

KEY RESOURCES FOR OUTCOME MEASUREMENTS

What can library staff do to improve program data collection, both qualitatively and quantitatively? I'm excited to report that several resources exist; here, I'll be discussing two that I've found to be outstanding. First, in 2015, the Public Library Association (PLA), a division of the American Library Association, designed Project Outcome—a powerful tool to assist librarians in improving data collection around programming. Second is the work of Gross, Mediavilla, and Walter in their book *5 Steps of Outcome-Based Planning & Evaluation for Youth Services*. While I'll be referencing the 2022 title, I utilized the 2009 publication (a much-loved, well-thumbed, and sticky note-peppered book) as the focus of my research methodology course at San José State University; I have found this resource and its updated title to be exceptional tools in helping create programs based on the library's mission and vision statements—having the end in mind is the key to effective program planning. The key question the librarian should ask is: What is the desired outcome of this children's program?

KEEPING THE GOAL IN MIND: PROJECT OUTCOME

As mentioned, this initiative was established in 2015 with the goal of providing public librarians with tools to help evaluate program offerings. The stated goal of Project Outcome is as follows:

> To help libraries understand and share the impact of essential library programs and services. As librarians, we see every day that library services put people on the path to literacy, technological know-how, or a better job—what we are often missing is the data to support it. Project Outcome provides simple tools and an easy-to-use process for measuring outcomes and collecting insights about all the ways we are meeting the needs of our communities. This understanding can improve the way libraries do business—from allocating existing resources more efficiently to advocating for new resources more effectively.[14]

This nice distinction helps librarians understand the nuances in data collection and the benefits of utilizing the Project Outcome toolkit: "Libraries commonly measure services in terms of 'how much we do,' focusing on the volume of outputs like the number of activities or services offered and number of patrons reached. Project Outcome seeks to capture the benefits (or outcomes) of library services in terms of 'what good we do,' like changes in library users' knowledge, confidence, behavior, or awareness. For example, while outputs may tell us how many library patrons attended a resumé-writing workshop, outcomes measurement can tell us whether those users feel more confident, informed, and equipped to seek a new job."[15]

Reading through the site offers a unique perspective on the need to take quantitative data further. The many offerings of this toolkit will help the library understand its own value in the community, but even more importantly, it will provide stakeholders with the necessary data to begin, continue, or increase library funding.

To utilize this toolkit, librarians need to establish an account, and once created, account holders are permitted to view all reports created for their own library, and multiple staff can have access to the surveys created by all who share the account as well as the data generated by those surveys. When I registered my library address and indicated Rye as my library, I immediately had access to several surveys completed by the director of the library. I highly recommend checking out the PLA Project Outcome site at https://www.projectoutcome.org/. Don't miss the clickable Impact Survey, initially developed by the University of Washington's Information School; its focus is patrons and their use of technology in the library.

PROJECT OUTCOME IN ACTION

Daniel Hensley reports on the Allen County Public Library's (ACPL) implementation of the Project Outcome Toolkit in his *Public Libraries Online* article entitled, "Work Smarter, Not Harder." Great success ensued when the library invested in staff training to reframe the view of the library and focus on a new "outward-facing approach to planning, service delivery, and evaluation."[16] Some of the key takeaways the ACPL reported were, first, that an investment of time is important in this sort of undertaking. Additionally, utilizing the resources of Project Outcome was key, but deep commitments of time and energy were needed for the process, especially when including this in strategic planning. Cherry-picking programs to survey rather than attempting to survey every program is an important element to ensure staff efficiency and avoid patrons feeling over-surveyed. Thinking of this process in terms of "a marathon, not a sprint" will ultimately be helpful as library programs and improvements can be considered over years. Finally, the ACPL outlines advice for users of Project Outcome that includes: "Don't survey everything, use a logic model to think through the process, give it time, consider an incentive, look at the results, make a plan about what you will do, follow up if you need to, and share the results with the community."[17] The RPL is approaching the time to develop its next strategic plan, and the information here will be useful to that end and useful to all libraries seeking to develop impactful strategic plans.

PROJECT OUTCOME: LOOKING AT IMPACTS

Published results of utilizing the Project Outcome toolkit bode well for libraries. Samantha Lopez, in "Project Outcome Results in Action," indicates that a primary advantage of utilizing this toolkit after an examination of five case studies by the PLA was the ability for libraries to "leverage their outcome data into actionable results. By using Project Outcome surveys, libraries are tracking their impact across time, improving and expanding programs and services to meet community needs, supporting new and deepening existing partnerships, and increasing library championship."[18] Advocacy in the library, particularly around children's services, has all too often been necessary. The Project Outcome initiative provides measurements to support needed advocacy.

OUTCOME-BASED PROGRAM PLANNING FOR YOUTH SERVICES

I mentioned the importance of Gross, Mediavilla, and Walter's work *5 Steps of Outcome-Based Planning and Evaluation for Youth Services* at the beginning of this chapter; I'll start here with a bit of history. This planning and evaluation model was established with an Institute of Museum and Library Services (IMLS) grant to the St. Louis Public Library with a subcontract to Florida State University. From this grant, Project CATE (Children's Access to and Use of Technology Evaluation) was developed, and outcome-based planning and evaluation (OBPE) ensued.[19]

While working on my MLIS degree at San José State Library's iSchool, I took the required Research Methodology Course and included the 2009 version of the text as the key to my project's focus; in fact, the text formed the foundation of my work. Submitted in 2012, this project changed the playing field for my program-planning process in youth services. I furnished my library director and board of trustees with the outline for a plan with the overarching desired outcome that LGBTIQ youth perceive the Rye Public Library as an organization of support and safety. This goal would be achieved through four programs, three of which had an outreach component, and the fourth involved librarian education in and around the New Hampshire seacoast area. Working my way through the older version of this book and beginning with my goal in mind, a new path for program planning was forged.

The elements of the Project CATE Outcome-Based Planning and Evaluation Model have been briefly outlined through my grad school project, but their importance cannot be stressed enough! I'm including the five-step approach of Gross, Mediavilla, and Walter to help you understand the detailed elements of this evaluation approach, and where pertinent, have included my own experience utilizing these steps. While this is an overview of the five steps, the book includes a chapter dedicated to each step, so detailed information is provided to help you achieve success in utilizing this method of program planning and evaluation.

STEP 1: GATHERING INFORMATION

The first step is gathering information—which includes an exploration of the library's strategic plans and mission and vision statements. As with other areas in this book in which I outline the importance of understanding the community, here, too, the authors detail understanding the community and assessing just what the community needs—that is, the community members you're attempting to reach.[20]

The following questions, according to Gross, Mediavilla, and Walter, are to be asked as you gather data:

- How does the library currently serve youth?
- Which other community organizations are also serving young people?
- What is known about the community's youth? What is life like for young people in the service area?

- What kind of information needs do youngsters have in your area? What kind of resources do they prefer? Do they have access to technology? How well developed are their information skills?[21]

STEP 2: DETERMINING OUTCOMES

Utilizing the information garnered in Step 1, outcomes are established that serve as the foundation for program development. Whether you are a new librarian or have years of experience, working with library colleagues to assist in this process and acting as a sounding board is beneficial for the process and builds connections. As a team, you can ensure that the program goals and intended outcomes align with Step 1 discoveries.

As with Step 1, the following questions quoted from Gross, Mediavilla, and Walter guide this next step in the process:

- What are the service and program priorities for youth in your service area?
- How can the library address those priorities?
- What kinds of outcomes should be the goal of program development?
- How will you know if your program achieves its outcome goals?[22]

STEP 3: DEVELOPING PROGRAMS AND SERVICES

Once baseline information is gathered and outcomes are determined, the development of programs and services forms the next step. While in this development phase, the library would do well to cast a large net in determining what services or programs already exist to avoid duplication. With the concept, I found that rather than merely creating programs around trends in the media or mirroring the programming in other libraries, this step focuses on program development from a more informed perspective after having completed the first two steps. Also noted by the authors—adopting an evaluation plan now is a good idea. Questions mentioned in the text for this step, and quoted here, are:

- What resources are available (in the library or local community) to help you design, implement, evaluate, and sustain your program or services?
- Do existing staff have the necessary skills to design, implement, and evaluate the program or service?
- Which community partners should be involved in the project?
- How can we best involve youth as key personnel in project design?[23]

STEP 4: CONDUCTING EVALUATIONS

I concur with the authors that, at least initially, this step in the process is more difficult and decidedly less fun than planning programs. However, after going through the process, I found it to be so impactful that it was worth doing and doing well. A good rule of thumb, according to Gross, Mediavilla, and Walter, is "asking you to think about assessing your program at the same time that you designate your outcome. If achievement of the proposed outcome seems impossible to measure, then modify your strategy so the outcome, program, and evaluation can realistically be accomplished."[24] This just makes good sense and was key to the success of my graduate school project.

STEP 5: LEVERAGING THE LIBRARY'S ROLE

I'll be discussing in subsequent chapters the need for youth services advocacy in the library; not all stakeholders necessarily believe or understand that programming and services the library offers have an impact on the community. This step ensures that you have the pertinent information that will clearly illustrate the library's value. As noted by Gross, Mediavilla, and Walter, "Nothing is more powerful than using community members' own words to describe their experience."[25] Share this information widely! With whom should these experiences be shared? The author's suggestions include "administration and governing bodies; funders and anyone who gave any kind of support to your project; the community in general; library staff; local schools and youth groups; community stakeholders in the welfare of youngsters; stakeholders interested in promoting the library; anyone else you can think of!"[26] Again, this advice is sensible and creates energy around the project, and the benefits derived from the positive connections are invaluable.

In short, I love and have fully embraced this model in my work. The immediate impact I've seen is the mindfulness with which I've planned programs, as well as the bond that developed among staff, youth, and the administration, who were all involved in the process. I'll discuss the value of collaboration between staff and managers in more detail in a later chapter, but with this graduate school project I undertook, I found it really brought people together. Additional outcomes are described in the book as well as much more detail of all aspects of the process. Utilizing this program planning and evaluation process can only help you work more efficiently by employing careful planning, and the benefits are vast and aren't fully mentioned here. Do yourself a favor and read this book cover to cover!

Much has been covered in this chapter, but the baseline is that program planning for children must find its footing in the library's goals, in the community itself, and before planning, these elements must be examined, considered, and incorporated to provide exemplary programming to the youth of the community. This program planning approach is thoughtful, provides multiple benefits, and ensures that programs truly serve youth according to their needs. No more of the "try everything and see what works" approach that I initially used in my early library career; everything changed, and through the outcomes, the youth department was more fully recognized for its value to the youth of the community.

REVIEW QUESTIONS

1. Examine the mission statement in the public library where you work, and if you're not in a public library, seek out this information from your town or city library. Assess the statement based on the criteria outlined in this chapter and include whether the statement is easily viewed by the public. Does the mission statement expressly include youth?
2. Does the library in which you work or your hometown or city library include a vision statement? How does this differ from the mission statement? Assess the statement based on the criteria in this chapter and mention whether this information is easily accessed by the public.
3. Does the library in which you work or your hometown or city library include a value statement? How does this differ from the mission or vision statements? Assess the statement based on the criteria in this chapter, and mention whether this information is easily accessed by the public.
4. Does your library have a strategic plan? If yes, outline the details of the plan.
5. Describe why the OBPE method described in *5 Steps to Outcome-Based Planning & Evaluation for Youth Services* is an important tool in youth services program planning.
6. Explain why you might sign yourself up for the Project Outcome Toolkit. Would this benefit your library? If yes, in what ways would this be beneficial?
7. When examining your children's programs over the last year, have you evaluated the results with both quantitative and qualitative measurements? How might you make changes/improvements to children's programming based on qualitative measures utilizing the methods discussed in this chapter?

NOTES

1. Michael Allison quoted in Sandra Hirsch, *Information Services Today: An Introduction*, 3rd ed. (Lanham, MD: Rowman & Littlefield, 2022), 259.
2. Webjunction, "Writing a Mission Statement," accessed November 5, 2022, https://www.webjunction.org/documents/webjunction/Writing_a_Mission_Statement.html.
3. Rye Public Library Board of Trustees, "Library Mission and Vision Statements," accessed November 12, 2022, https://ryepubliclibrary.org/library-mission-statements/.
4. Ibid., 1.
5. Julia Martins, "How to Write a Vision Statement: Steps and Examples," accessed November 12, 2022, https://asana.com/resources/vision-statement.

6. Rye Public Library Board of Trustees, "Library Mission and Vision Statements."
7. Rye Public Library Board of Trustees, "Strategic Plan 2012–2015," accessed December 18, 2022, https://www.dropbox.com/s/r9ut1cqs88hnetw/RPLthreeyearstrategicplan2012-2015.pdf?dl=0.
8. Fullstory, "Qualitative vs. Quantitative Data: What's the Difference?," accessed December 23, 2022, https://www.fullstory.com/blog/qualitative-vs-quantitative-data/.
9. Ibid.
10. New Hampshire State Library, "Public Library Statistics / Complete Library Statistics," accessed December 18, 2022, https://www.nh.gov/nhsl/lds/public_library_stats.html.
11. Pia Margaret Gahagan and Philip James Calvert, "Evaluating a Public Library Makerspace," *Public Library Quarterly* 39, no. 4 (May 2019): 323, Taylor & Francis Online.
12. Ibid., 323.
13. Ibid., 341.
14. Public Library Association, "Project Outcome," accessed December 18, 2022, https://www.ala.org/pla/data/performancemeasurement.
15. Ibid.
16. Daniel Hensley, "Work Smarter Not Harder," *Public Libraries Online*, accessed December 18, 2022, https://publiclibrariesonline.org/2020/11/work-smarter-not-harder/.
17. Ibid.
18. Samantha Lopez, "Project Outcome Results in Action," *Public Library Quarterly* 37, no. 2 (January 2018): 151, Taylor & Francis Online.
19. Melissa Gross, Cindy Mediavilla, and Virginia A. Walter, *5 Steps of Outcome-Based Planning and Evaluation for Youth Services* (Chicago: ALA Editions, 2022), x.
20. Ibid., 26.
21. Ibid., 26–27.
22. Ibid., 27.
23. Ibid., 28.
24. Ibid., 29.
25. Ibid., 29.
26. Ibid., 29–30.

3

Storytime and Children's Programming

Midnight Walking Tacos, Noodle Storytimes, and Harry Potter in 99 Seconds. Sound intriguing? These are some of the most popular programs I held for youth in the public library. While the taco and Harry Potter programs were both aimed at an older crowd, for illustrative purposes, I'm including them here. In fact, I had third and fourth graders memorizing the "Harry Potter in 99 Seconds" song and singing at volume; it was a main feature for several weeks of our Harry Potter Club program, and the kids loved how the Harry Potter canon was summarized in this short and catchy song. Midnight Walking Tacos was a "lock in" program I held for my Teen Advisory Board, but it could easily be featured for younger patrons: Crush chips in an individual-sized bag of Doritos, add taco components, and eat right out of the bag. Walking tacos are a catchy and creative way to draw kids to a program, plus including food is always a draw. Lastly, Noodle Storytime? Laurie Berkner helped make this event successful as I included her song "Victor Vito." Who doesn't want to eat spaghetti with Freddie? Check out both songs mentioned here; they're easily found online. From these three examples, it's clear that common factors in all successful programming are creativity and fun. In addition, however, elements connecting programming to literacy in some ways are also needed, and this was included in my planning; more on this in an upcoming section.

    Children's programming is at the heart of children's library services. Aside from providing a robust collection of books, offering programming is the key to a vibrant youth department. At the core of children's programming is storytime—I love storytime! I can't say that was always true; when I first began in the youth department, I had been working with middle school-aged students, so storytime was initially quite unfamiliar, and I was not in my comfort zone. After a few months, though, I began to fully embrace this programming and looked forward to the weekly half-hour with joy. To begin, I sought out fellow youth librarians in the area who offered storytime and I arranged with them to observe their work. The key takeaway for me was the exuberance and enthusiastic approach librarians brought to the program; in turn, children responded with excitement and smiles and were clearly having a great time. After offering the toddler storytime, a program already in place when I began in the youth department, I expanded beyond the program to include baby storytime and an assortment of specialty storytimes, like pajama storytime and stuffie sleepover events.

In addition to looking at storytime in its various forms, I'll discuss programming in multiple formats, general programming, and virtual programming. The age groups of storytime examined here are baby, toddler, preschool, and school-aged storytimes, as well as a quick review of family storytimes. While storytime lies at the heart of library offerings, summer reading is a vital program that becomes richer when partnering with local schools. Summer reading helps kids avoid the "summer slide" and keeps kids engaged and excited about reading after school's out. That said, the summer reading program is such an important element within a librarian's annual programming that I will only mention it here but will explore it more deeply in chapter 4.

STORYTIME

THE NUTS AND BOLTS OF STORYTIME: DEFINING AND PLANNING

Before looking closely at storytime and its working parts, a definition is in order. One I find particularly helpful for being succinct and complete comes from Katie Fitzgerald in *Storytime Success: A Practical Guide for Librarians*: "Today's story times are dynamic performances, including not just stories, but also a variety of extension activities and props designed to engage children and caregivers alike."[1] I'll be mentioning the importance of the word "dynamic" throughout this section. The librarian is effectively "on stage" and is performing to and engaging with the children in attendance, and to be effective, this performance is filled with excitement, enthusiasm, fun, laughter, smiles, and positivity. To be confident of your abilities as a performer is something that will grow over time unless you're a natural, but careful planning and understanding of your audience will ensure that you include the perfect combination of activities, reading, movement, and songs to engage caregivers and children. In time, you will embrace your inner thespian, and once the first book is opened for you to read, you'll say to yourself, *Let the show begin!*

To be sure, I've attended storytimes in which the librarian is the opposite of playful and is instead rigid and requires children to sit still and be quiet while stories are read; in this scenario, a kind of verbal punishment is given when kids "act out." This approach is ineffective, potentially damaging to children, discourages attendance at future programs, and is outdated. Research has shown that engagement—a two-way communication between storytime provider and children—is the effective approach.

The importance of active engagement was driven home for me in Meagan Dowd Lambert's book *Reading Picture Books with Children: How to Shake Up Storytime and Get Kids Talking About What They See*. The Whole Book Approach, "a co-constructive (interactive) storytime model centered on the picture book as an art form,"[2] constructed by Lambert, seeks to simply read books *with* children rather than *to* them. To further define this approach, Lambert expounds, noting that "During Whole Book storytimes, children's active participation in making meaning of all they see and hear during a picture book takes precedence over moving through the pages at the pace of the adult's oral reading of the text."[3] She further explains that there is no prescription for exact storytimes but to embrace an organic interaction that invites children to take in the whole of the book—"its art, design, production, paratextual and textual elements—in ways that feel natural and enriching to them and to you as the adult reader."[4] Lambert's book itself takes this to heart and includes margin notes that describe itself with terms like serif typeface, pull quote, verso page, and more.[5] A delight-filled look at storytime, don't miss checking out Lambert's book for yourself.

STORYTIME MUSTS

First, to set the stage, you want to convey your love of books and how you want to share your enthusiasm with the children visiting your library. To help you prepare, ask yourself what books *you* love, what instruments do *you* play, and what kind of music gets *you* moving. Find your inner child, recall the past, and connect to that energy and enthusiasm. Beginning here ensures that you convey to young patrons your sense of connection and excitement with the storytime elements, and this elevates your storytime from a decent offering to one that shines. Do you love classical, jazz, or swing music? Find a way to bring it in. How about puppets, dogs, flowers, or crafting? Any activity or favorite foods—they can all act as fodder for your storytime that easily translates to fun engagement.

Another important aspect of storytime is to be flexible, expect the unexpected, and be ready for instant adjustments. Learning to "read the room" is vital for any age group. Knowing when to stretch an activity, engage your audience with questions, or just take a moment to breathe is critical to the success of any storytime. Over time and watching others you can learn the skills to engage the children and their caretakers, what props will help elevate the storytime, and how to utilize a variety of creative methods to keep kids engaged. Please note that there is so much available online; you're not alone, and you're not creating storytimes in a vacuum. Check out what other folks do and adapt the ideas for yourself. Browsing through the incredible resources online, especially at jbrary.com, you'll benefit; they include theme ideas, videos, and an archive that will provide storytime options for the rest of your career. This is just one of many online storytime resources to explore.

Finally, know that not all picture books make great read-alouds; you'll want to do some research online, but really, you need to read, read, read! Read picture books every day. Get a sense of the rhythm of the words, the messages, and the elements to which kids will connect. Try them out in smaller groups informally; perhaps try an informal reading session when a child visits the library—ask if you can read them a story and note their reactions. As far as favorites, I have found several, including nearly any title by Julia Donaldson; she has perfected the rhythm of rhyme, making her books like *Room on the Broom*, *The Gruffalo*, and *Stick Man* excellent storytime choices.

STORYTIME ELEMENTS AND PLANNING FOR FUN

While specific elements of storytime are included for various groups of kids, consideration should be taken to offer appropriate activities and books for age and developmental needs. I'll address this within each age group, but I'm beginning here with common elements—the plan or outline that follows is appropriate for toddlers to preschool-aged children.

This is the storytime structure that I grew to adopt over time; it worked for a 20- to 30-minute session. This is a kind of outline, but bear in mind that flexibility is key! You may or may not get to all the carefully designed plans you've made, and that's okay!

STORYTIME: MY BASIC STRUCTURE

1. Welcome song and theme of the day's storytime
2. Greeting, introductions, and ground rules
3. Feature book
4. Fingerplay
5. Interactive song
6. Second book
7. Movement activity
8. Third book
9. Closing song
10. Craft
11. Free play and parent interaction time

I begin storytime with my welcome song; it gets the attention of children and caregivers and marks the start of storytime. The welcome song I sang was always the same, and kids loved the sign language that went with it. I used "Hello, Friends," which included sign language for "hello," "friends," "time," and "say." Familiarity is the key, so doing the same song over and over gives the kids an element of connection and recognition. As with nearly all I'm mentioning, this song is easily found online, along with sign language you can include.

Next, and very importantly, is the introduction of yourself and any helpers, the introduction of the storytime, and the acknowledgment and welcoming of participants verbally. Letting the group know that moving around, leaving for restroom breaks—it's all okay with you. In this way, you've established a more freeing atmosphere and have set some "ground rules."

After greeting and welcoming participants, I would typically introduce the theme or focus of the day's storytime, such as a barnyard or animal theme. For this example, I might tell the children we're going to have fun barking like dogs and mooing like cows! Including bridge conversations like this between the storytime elements helps you connect the activity or song back to your focus and links from whatever you've just done to the next part of storytime.

A little about repetition is in order here. I always included the welcome song above for all age groups. Depending on the age of the group, I might include not only the same song but also the same book. Learning something for the first time is great, but the feeling you get when you know all the words to a song provides a sense of belonging, which also allows participants to, for many kids, sing their song with gusto; the same goes for repeating books. Kids' enthusiasm is very contagious, and even newcomers will feel the warmth and fervor of the group as they join in song and book recognition. Don't be afraid to repeat favorite songs or books at storytimes, because along with that sense of belonging comes mastery, one goal of storytime and early literacy.

As I've mentioned, storytime may, but doesn't necessarily have to, take on a theme, such as the animal theme outlined here. If I did choose a theme, I'd build the storytime around a "focus" book. A title that I loved and knew would be an especially excellent read-aloud is the timeless picture book *Bark, George* by Jules Feiffer. In *Bark, George*, George the dog makes some strange sounds because of what he has ingested—*oink, moo*, and so on. His mother is worried and brings him to the vet; hilarity ensues as the dog clearly makes sounds that are not barks, and having kids guess what the vet will pull out of George makes this title engaging and fun; older children will get the funny twist at the end. At times, I even followed up with a video presentation of the book, the Scholastic Video Collection entitled *Bark, George and More Doggie Tails*.

This title would inspire songs, activities, and movement, including fun animal fingerplays easily found on the Internet. You might create little props for your fingerplay, but just your hand will do the trick. A fingerplay element is a kind of rhyme that sometimes involves counting and learning numbers in a fun way. An example is the old "Five Little Monkeys Jumping on the Bed" choice. Simply count down with your fingers the number of monkeys left after each iteration of the verse.

From there, I would choose a song or two connecting to animals or dogs, and for this, I might select Laurie Berkner's "Pig on Her Head." I once created a headband with a comical pink foam pig attached; kids passed it around and danced excitedly as I played the guitar and sang the name of each child in the group. It was great fun. Interactive songs get kids moving and excited about storytime. I cannot stress enough the value of both Raffi and Laurie Berkner for music. Even if you don't sing, you can play the songs, but really, kids don't care if you have a great voice; they'll just jump right in and sing along with you. Remember, your enthusiasm is key. If you don't have a personal investment in the material you're presenting, your young patrons will know and will likely not engage as much. Jump around, sing loudly, act silly, and get them involved! Berkner and Raffi are oldies but goodies; explore more to find great storytime songs for kids—perhaps even a local group that performs for kids.

Next, share a second book. At this point in the storytime program, you will have noted how engaged your young audience and their caregivers are, and you can adjust if needed. Perhaps the group can't focus on heavy text—you might just get the kids to comment on the pictures by asking them to tell the story from what they see. Many creative approaches can be effective. For this animal-themed storytime, I might include *What the Ladybug Heard* by Julia Donaldson. This story has many things going for it: it rhymes, it's hilarious, and it's engaging. The one drawback is that it is long. Gauge your audience—can they hold out for a story this long? Or would it be better to abandon reading the book and jump to the next program element, a movement activity? To bridge this activity, I might say, "Remember George? What kind of animal is George?" Kids will likely yell out, "a DOG!" I'd say, "Yes, George is a dog, and now we're going to act like George!" It takes finesse to connect to the needs of the kids, but this comes with time. You just need to know you have permission to adjust any time it's needed.

In keeping with the animal theme, a movement activity would likely include acting like an animal most kids know, such as a dog, cat, or pig, and so on. You may have to do two movement activities in a row if your audience requires this kind of engagement. For this part of storytime, I'd start with, "If you're a dog and you know it clap your hands; if you're a dog and you know it bark out loud, then wag your tail, run around, sit up and beg." Get kids acting like dogs—let it be loud, let them run around and have fun! Remember, it's very important that you also need to do these motions with enthusiasm—find your inner dog and let it go! If you show the kids you're having fun, they'll have fun, and their caregivers will have fun. At first you may feel uncomfortable, but you'll see the impact your infectious enthusiasm has when you see smiles, giggles, and laughter from the children. This will likely encourage even the shyest librarians to step out of their comfort zone.

One important element in a movement activity is calming down your audience and bringing the activity to a close. Putting your dogs to bed with exaggerated yawns is one method. End with, "Now all you puppies, get in your bed and go to sleep," and demonstrate lying down like a puppy in a blanket.

After a few moments of rest, you should once again gauge the group to assess their mood. If they are restless, ask them to share what they liked about the program, then using that information, sing another song, dance, or repeat a movement exercise. Incredibly, some groups of kids are quite mellow, having enjoyed their rest and prefer the quiet of another story or two. I've held storytimes where the kids insisted on just having stories and we skipped the other activities, but those were rare!

If you've determined that your group is ready for their third and final book, perhaps consider engaging the help of a puppet to read the book; introducing another element can get kids excited about the next story. If your group is especially ready to hang out and listen, a funny title I liked was *Amos: The Story of an Old Dog and His Couch*. This one is best for a very mellow group; it's longer and requires a bit more of the children's attention. If you can't make it through the whole book, select fewer pages to tell the story and engage the children in their thoughts as the book is read. Also, if you have a helper puppet tell the story, such as your favorite cow puppet, this will likely be engaging enough to get to the end of the book.

Storytime is over at this point, so signaling that is the closing song. I sang "Goodbye, Friends," which was identical to the opening song, so there was some recognition as I subbed in the word "goodbye." After the song, I thanked everyone for being at storytime, reminded them we'd be happy to help them find books in the library, and mentioned upcoming programs they might be interested in. I then invited them to head over to the craft.

The storytime craft is the final focus and will vary depending on the age of the group. As mentioned, there are a plethora of ideas online—seek them out and adapt at will! Pinterest is your friend, believe me. For this final element of my example storytime, all supplies were prepared ahead of time and were ready for kids to get right to work. In this example, I'd have children work on creating a brown lunch bag "George" dog with an opening for the mouth. Kids would decorate their George bag, then color and cut out images of the animals that George swallows. Younger children may need help with scissors from their caregivers.

Lastly, but not the least important, is time for children to play and interact with one, another along with time for caregivers to engage. Providing toys allows children to engage while caregivers chat with each other and with you. This final portion of storytime provides community connections and is integral to the mission of the public library. Be sure to include this important component in your storytime and announce the specifics to caregivers as part of the storytime marketing. One thing to note—be sure you're not so busy cleaning up storytime supplies that you don't take this time to interact informally with the kids and caregivers. It's the best time to make connections and check in about programming needs or anything else caregivers may want to share with you.

MY TIPS FOR SUCCESSFUL STORYTIMES

- Remember to engage the group; ask questions about images in the book, their opinions, and their predictions about what's coming next. Ask them about colors on the page or the number of animals depicted. Don't stick solely to reading—ask them their thoughts.
- Learn to read sideways or upside down! You'll need to show kids the pictures in the book, and really, if you can include a book or two each time that is oversized, all the better! I've successfully included the Big Books like *Rosie Walks*, *The Very Hungry Caterpillar*, and *Brown Bear, Brown Bear, What Do You See?* Resting these on your feet and reading upside down is the way to go.
- Create a book display in your storytime area. Set up several titles around the theme that kids can check out if they'd like.
- Make the space comfortable. I always included large pillows for kids to sit on and would bring in a warm nightlight, lamp, glowing moon, or some item to create a "home-like" feeling.
- Invite caregivers to also engage by including them in the songs and other activities.
- Use puppets with wild abandon! You might just do all your speaking and reading through a puppet. You may have dialogue with the puppet about what he or she thought of the book, then ask children to also engage by answering the same questions.
- While the structure I mention here is great to adopt when you're first beginning to offer storytime in your career, each librarian will find his or her own formula to provide outstanding service to children in the library. I encourage you to bust out of the box and forge your own path to success!
- Flannel boards are another excellent addition to storytime; they create a visual connection to the story or rhyme you're performing. A flannel board is essentially a sandwich board covered in flannel; animals and shapes that align with the storytime theme are cut from flannel and are "stuck" to the flannel board. Get creative here and expand your flannel board use—the possibilities are endless, and a quick Internet search will yield images for ideas.

STORYTIMES FROM BIRTH TO AGE FIVE

When planning a storytime, the first consideration is the age group of the young patrons. Children are typically grouped into four categories: babies (birth to around eighteen months), toddlers (ages eighteen to thirty-six months), preschool (ages three to five years), and school-aged children (grades one through three). Note that family storytimes are likely to include a wider variety of ages from birth up to age eleven; there is more to come on the dynamics needed for this mixed-age group.

As has been discussed, children from birth through toddlers are at different developmental stages, so care should be taken to ensure that the content of the storytime aligns with the proper developmental stage. In addition to age levels, assessing competency is also helpful in planning; this might initially be a challenging assessment to make, but it is easier with time. The concept of scaffolding, or determining different levels of support, comes into play here. According to Saroj Nadkarni Ghoting and Kathy Fling Klatt, "Scaffolding is an educational term for the process of adjusting the level of assistance to fit the child's abilities. More support is offered when a task is new; less is provided as the child's competence increases, thereby increasing the child's independence and mastery."[6] A keen understanding of where children are developmentally and how fresh the content is that is presented to them is a sound practice for librarians to follow so that they might better meet children's needs.

STORYTIME FOR BABIES

As I noted earlier, my comfort level working with storytime-aged children was hard won; teaching junior high students how to diagram a sentence could not be more different than presenting a thirty-minute program to wee ones. So it was with the baby storytime. Still, it didn't take long to overcome the butterflies in my stomach thanks to the smiles on those little faces along with the enthusiasm and engagement of the caregivers that brought me a deep sense of joy. Inherent in the work is the satisfaction of watching nonverbal infants develop during weekly program attendance and eventually sing and participate. Baby storytime became a cornerstone of my storytime offerings, and I attribute much of this success to the Mother Goose on the Loose (MGOL) approach. Attending an American Library Association (ALA) conference in Chicago one year, I had the chance to meet Betsy Diamant-Cohen, creator of MGOL, and I was awestruck—as though I had just met a rock star. She is a rock star in the baby storytime world! In fact, Betsy won the Distinguished Service award in 2022 from the ALA's Association for Library Service to Children.[7]

THE MOTHER GOOSE ON THE LOOSE METHOD

The *Mother Goose on the Loose* manual is a comprehensive resource that includes learning the system as well as an invitation to personalize the "baby lapsit" program. Caregivers hold the child during the program and interact throughout. There are so many options for all elements of baby storytime, including rhymes, songs, and even how to narrate various portions of the storytime. Perhaps the best offering is the inclusion of ten ready-to-present programs; I found that with just a minimal investment of time, I could start the program right away and read through the *Mother Goose on the Loose* manual at my leisure to round out and perfect various elements. It's that simple. In addition to this excellent resource, more materials can be found on mgol.net, and I recommend subscribing to the newsletter, which provides up-to-date information on childhood development and other news. There is even a section on the website addressing virtual programming.

Baby storytime using the award-winning MGOL approach is comprised of ten segments and utilizes an 80 percent repetition formula for use from week to week.[8] The goals of the program are to provide research-based early literacy coupled with traditional storytime elements that inform developmental activities and to model these entertaining elements for caregiver engagement to allow for bonding time with the child. Target ages for the program are birth to age three.[9] Diamant-Cohen's program is based on the "Listen, Like, Learn" teaching approach of Barbara Cass-Beggs and includes many of Cass-Beggs's original songs; the focus is on emergent literacy, which is the time between birth and the time a child can read and write—knowledge and skills that are learned before first grade.[10] Important to note are the "Markers of emergent literacy in babies which include an 'awareness' of:

- Vocabulary: knowing names of things
- Print and motivation: learning basic rules of written language and showing an interest in and enjoyment of books
- Writing: making a variety of marks that can range from circular, horizontal, separate scribble markers to letter-like forms or actual letters
- Phonemics: being able to hear and manipulate the smaller sounds in words"[11]

To achieve that early literacy, MOGL utilizes nine teaching elements outlined here.[12] They include the following, along with my own experiences; when quotations are included, they are noted:

- Repetition—this is comforting for young children and helps them feel connected to the event.
- Ritual—like repetition, ritual activities help participants feel a sense of stability; examples include songs for both the opening and closing of the storytime, or simply repeating any element in the same place each time.
- A Fun, Positive Environment—I can't stress this enough, and it's being repeated here for emphasis. According to Barbara Frederickson in Diamant-Cohen, "Environment affects the mind, body, and spirit. Studies have shown that sensory-enriched environments have the power to improve stress management, immune systems, emotional stability, emotional adaptation, memory and learning, behavior and life extension."[13] My experience bears this out; children engage when they are enjoying themselves.
- Play—there is no separation between learning and play; in fact, noted by Stuart Brown in Diamant-Cohen, "As children play, connections in their

brains are formed between what they are doing, what they think and feel about what they are doing, and what they are discovering as they are doing that particular thing."[14]
- Being Read To—the reading life of children is shaped early, and modeling reading by caregivers and librarians lends itself to feeling good about reading; they'll feel safe and comfortable, and because of that feeling, they'll want it to happen often.
- Movement—movement is critical because, as Cohen-Diamant cites Carla Hannaford, "Physical activity can actually create physiological changes in the brain. Movement accelerates heart rates and can also correlate with increased attention levels. Greater attention often leads to greater memory performance. Movement activates the limbic system, which leads to the brain receiving increased sensory information and creating an emotional tone in which memory works more effectively."[15] In around 2006 when I first began honing my storytime skills, I believed that movement activities were included to help "control" the child and provide him or her with these activities so the rest of storytime would allow them to relax and listen. Although this is confirmed in Cohen-Diamant, she also notes that permitting physical movement lends itself to a myriad of benefits.
- Music—many benefits are derived from children experiencing music, and among them, "children learn rhyme, timbre, and tone. They learn concepts such as high and low, soft and loud, and fast and slow. They learn how to use their voices as musical instruments and connect with others through singing."[16]
- Time to Relax—The lullaby element in MGOL permits both children and caregivers much-needed time to unwind and just breathe. Diamant-Cohen states that this time allows the children to process and retain what they've just experienced in storytime, and it models lullabies for the caregivers to help their children relax.
- Appeal to Multiple Intelligences—finally, the multiple activities presented in MGOL will likely find at least one of the eight intelligences outlined by Howard Gardner: "(1) logical-mathematical (math and logic skills), (2) musical (keenly aware of rhythm, pitch, melody, tone, etc.; it may include musical talent to sing, play an instrument, or conduct), (3) spatial (being able to perceive, manipulate, and recreate aspects of the visual-spatial world; thinking in pictures), (6) intrapersonal (self-intelligence), (7) interpersonal (social intelligence), and (8) naturalist (the intelligence of making distinctions in the world of nature)."[17]

This recounting of the MGOL program is among many approaches to baby storytime in the same way I presented a structure for your overall storytimes in the previous section. You might find similar programs referred to by many names, including other baby lapsit programs; creative librarians use catchy names to draw patrons to the library; check out some of the catchy titles at mclskids.pbworks.com under the Storytime Names tab. Some included there are *Baby Jamboree, Baby Bouncers, Little Listeners,* and *Romp and Rhyme.*[18]

Baby storytime is beneficial in so many ways for your community. Kate, a parent who brought both her children to my MGOL program, noted that both her children loved the songs and music and the lollipop drum (I had a fantastic drum for the "rum pum pum, this is my drum" segment). She said, "I loved the community that brought young families together. It was a saving grace for me to get out of the house and a great introduction to the library for my kids."[19] Including a baby storytime at the library is highly recommended and could very possibly become your own cornerstone program!

TODDLER STORYTIME

Toddler storytime presents very differently from our lapsit program outlined in the previous section; the following are my observations and knowledge gained over time in reading about children's development.

Most toddlers at this age (eighteen to thirty-six months) are mobile! Not only are these children mobile, but they *need* to move. Toddler storytime is busy as children in this age bracket are inquisitive and enjoy allowances to explore the room, dance and move freely, and interact with fellow storytime participants. For some time during my toddler storytimes, I felt like a failure when these toddlers were running around and playing as I performed stories, fingerplays, and waved scarves over my head. I soon learned that staying still and listening attentively to a story was not required for toddlers to take in what was happening. As an example, I was so intent on having toddlers become engaged with my program that I became ridiculously enthusiastic, overly so, and tried all kinds of actions to get children's attention. In fact, in observing other storytimes in the region, I thought the same thing—the librarian as a performer was simply not good enough to keep children's attention. Explaining my perceived failure to a fellow librarian, she let me in on her understanding of toddler development: Despite their movement and engagement around the room, they were, in fact, taking it all in. When I learned this, I began to observe that children who had been in motion at a previous storytime could sing a song that they had previously seemed to ignore. Relief!

In addition to mobility, children at this developmental stage are becoming more independent and seek to do things on their own. "I can do it myself" is a common phrase heard at this age. Children in this age group are exploring their world as they adopt a keen sense of self; they are striving for independence and prefer to act on their own to accomplish tasks. You may have heard the concept that children at this age truly think they are the center of the universe. Incorporating activities that play to that need for independence will ensure a fun storytime. Note that if you've worked with children, a common word used at this age is "mine," so I try to provide props for each child, though having to share is a great option to offer on occasion. An additional storytime element I include with this age group is helping clean up after activities and at the end of storytime before heading for the craft. At this stage, caregivers are still present and can assist children with cleanup.

Finally, a few last mental and social skills present themselves in the toddler group: children at this age can use their imaginations more fully, so anything in your storytime related to pretending will be welcome and fun. Also, toddler attention spans are short, so shorter books are probably best. Toddlers are still learning right from wrong and have developing awareness of other people, particularly other children, and their caregivers. Helping them recognize and address fellow participants by acknowledging children and their caregivers by name is an excellent practice.

The storytime format presented at the beginning of this section is an excellent beginning outline for the structure of toddler storytime. As with all sections mentioned in this chapter, entire books are written on the many elements of storytime—from age groups to formats to titles on including music in storytime. The treatment intended here is an outline and can be expanded upon significantly. Explore the world of storytime by checking out books on the topic that appeal to you, especially those that focus on areas in which you may feel a lack of confidence.

PRESCHOOL STORYTIME

While toddlers are finding their feet, preschool children—those aged three to five years old—have gained better mastery of motor skills. So, for example, you may find that children in this group are able to use scissors in the storytime craft without help from their caregivers. (And often, they want to show you and others how they can do things by themselves!) Preschool children also exhibit more independence, and friendships are formed at this age. The librarian can present somewhat longer stories as children's attention spans are increased. Kids at this stage love being helpers, so the librarian might select a child or children to help hand out props, hold a book, or help turn the page. Vocabulary is dramatically increased, and you may find children wanting to tell their own story—in fact, soliciting stories from children is another way to connect them to the storytime. As a sidenote, children love to read to each other and to pets, and even non-readers will happily tell the story by interpreting the pictures as the dog quietly listens—it's adorable. For years, I had a successful program where children could sign up to read to one of the library's four-legged friends—a very sweet lab that children could cuddle with and read to; it was a great hit. Because children at this age ask many questions, honoring this and soliciting questions is another great way to make your storytimes all-encompassing. Finally, the sense of play and pretending are developed even further, so playing to those interests, as with toddler storytime, is a nice inclusion.

The basic storytime plan outlined earlier in this chapter is also appropriate for preschool. Naturally, the older the child becomes, the more sophisticated the content of storytime will become. Note the abilities of children in each stage, but remember that even children at this age have favorite activities they encountered in their younger years at storytime and enjoy singing those songs, hearing those books, or reliving other activities from their toddler days or earlier. I often include some of the activities from baby storytime and watch their faces light up with acknowledgment, providing recognition and a sense of accomplishment. Their smiles will once again confirm their love for recognition.

SCHOOL-AGED STORYTIME

While it's possible to hold school-aged storytimes at the library, in my experience, I did not hold regular storytimes for this age group but rather took the opportunity to do some outreach. I've had excellent collaborations with teachers at the local elementary school and had so much fun heading to the classroom for stories; from my own experience as a teacher, having someone come into the classroom on a Friday afternoon—after a long week—and read stories to the students was a godsend. I typically arranged to meet with grades K–3 at least once a month at staggered times on a Friday afternoon. I must say, this was a favorite outreach activity of mine.

Book selections for this age group can be more sophisticated, and having a storytime in the classroom ensures that kids are pretty much attentive. I often selected at least one very humorous book (a favorite that has never lost its luster is the 2014 *The Book with No Pictures* by B.J. Novak) and tried to bring in books that tied to the curriculum but were perhaps less instructive than what kids might be reading in the classroom. In addition to the books I'd read with children, I brought along some they might like to check out themselves and was always sure to mention other programs happening at the library for their age group.

FAMILY STORYTIME

Admittedly, there is overlap in this area as many libraries offer storytimes for the family but limit the age groups to under two, under five, and so on. At my family storytimes, the entire family is welcome, so children of all ages may be present. Some infants, toddlers, preschoolers, or even older children may attend, but they are typically not older than eleven. The key is to offer something for the entire family while integrating familiar elements from the basic storytime plan. One recommendation to help you plan for your family storytime is to require program registration. This way you'll have a better idea of who is coming and what the ages of the children will be so that you might plan your elements better.

Aside from providing children with storytime, family storytime also gives caregivers a model on which to base their own interactions with their children—to foster a love of books to provide school readiness, language development, and a love for lifelong learning; children also see their caregivers participating and experience family activities as fun; it is wonderful to see how bonds within the family are built.

It's fun for kids to attend "special" storytimes for school-aged children at the library. I had great success with pajama storytime. Choosing an evening time shortly after the standard dinner time, I set up a cozy atmosphere for kids who arrived in their jammies; naturally, I had on my jammies, slippers, and a robe as well. Including a fun nightlight helped set the tone for this more subdued series of books. Because children were put to bed shortly after this storytime, I structured it so that more engaging and energy-filled stories and activities happened first, and the last book was usually about falling asleep or sleeping or dreaming. You get the idea.

To be confident of your abilities as a performer is something you will likely develop over time, but careful planning for and an understanding of your audience will ensure that you include the perfect combination of activity, reading, movement, engagement, and song to engage caregivers and children.

OTHER STORYTIME CONSIDERATIONS

DRAG STORY HOUR

Before examining the reception of Drag Story Hour in libraries, here's a snippet of history about the founding of the project. According to Wikipedia, Drag Story Hour found roots in San Francisco in 2015 and was created by Michelle Tea, who saw the need after bringing her infant son to the library. Although library staff were welcoming and accepting of Michelle as a queer parent, she found the content heteronormative and wanted to offer more inclusive and affirming programming.[20] Drag Story Hour states on its website that "Drag Story Hour celebrates reading through the glamorous art of drag. Our chapter network creates diverse, accessible, and culturally inclusive family programming where kids can express their authentic selves and become bright lights of change in their communities."[21] In answer to the question of what Drag Story Hour is, the site states, "It's just what it sounds like! Storytellers using the art of drag to read books to kids in libraries, schools, and bookstores. DSH captures the imagination and play of the gender fluidity of childhood and gives kids glamorous, positive, and unabashedly queer role models. In spaces like this, kids can see people who defy rigid gender restrictions and imagine a world where everyone can be their authentic selves!"[22]

Anecdotally, I have heard nothing but positive reception from my colleagues who have offered the programming. They shared that the number of participants exceeded expectations and both caregivers and children were enthusiastic and excited during the story hour; many children arrived in high spirits dressed in frocks peppered with glitter and color—truly embracing the spirit of the event.

With the enthusiasm around the positive impacts of Drag Story Hour shared by colleagues, I've also read extensively about those who oppose its presence in the library. There are far too many incidents to convey here, but as recently as December 2022, protestors gathered outside the New York Public Library Jackson Heights branch in Queens and were met by a far greater number of counter-protestors. Though no physical violence ensued, vitriol was openly spewed, and it wasn't apparent whether arrests were made.[23] Most of the argument against Drag Story Hour appears to be around the concept that children are being groomed and sexualized, but counter-protesters state that the storytimes are about acceptance and freedom of expression. Additionally, critics also claim that the story hours promote gender confusion, but those who welcome the story hour noted, according to Katie Gillespie, that the children see through the negativity and just see love.[24]

INCLUDING RACE IN STORYTIME

Librarian Jessica Bratt, currently the Community Engagement Coordinator at the Grand Rapids Public Library, is among those at the forefront of the movement to educate the library community about including race in storytime. Her 2022 book *Let's Talk About Race in Storytimes* provides an excellent understanding of the issues around how race has been treated, or rather, not traditionally treated, in storytimes as well as providing not only diverse titles but also outlining practical steps to take for success. Bratt's website, whimsylibrarian.com, is another abundantly helpful resource; here, Bratt offers workshops and training for "equipping librarians with the tools to talk about race with young children and caregivers in library storytimes. She uses an anti-oppression framework that is adaptable for educators, caregivers, and other nonprofit sectors."[25] In a guest post on the jbrary.com site, Bratt outlines reasoning for doing self-work around race and offers five questions to ponder:

1. Who am I?
2. What are my self interests? (sic)
3. Who are my people?
4. Who am I accountable to?
5. What am I best positioned to do?[26]

This self-work is important to move forward in talking about race in storytime. These and other steps provide librarians with the tools needed beyond merely including diverse books in the library collection. Check out the resources mentioned and make a commitment to becoming a lifelong learner who embraces cultural humility while striving for cultural competence.

GENERAL PROGRAMMING

We've examined many facets of storytime, but the public library offers much more in the way of programming for youth of all ages. In this section, I've highlighted some successful programming I've done, the benefits of programming in multiple formats, virtual programs, and a brief look at programming budgets.

Before embarking on the journey of program planning, know that you need to establish a few parameters first. Consider undertaking a self-assessment at the library you work in or one you utilize most. Begin with a look at what's already being offered at the library. Note whether there are any age groups who have more or fewer offerings than others and seek to fill in gaps. Review attendance records for the various programs; what draws more participants? Notice programs that didn't have such a great attendance. Naturally, how you define a decent turnout will vary for each program and for each community, but use common sense. Reviewing your programs provides a starting point for planning.

As mentioned extensively in chapter 2, planning with the result in mind is critical, and to aid your planning, widen your programming assessment to better understand offerings in your community. Search your town, city, or region to determine what is out there for kids. Is there a skatepark in town? How about surfing lessons, movie theatres, playgrounds, hiking trails, or anything else kids are enjoying? Knowing what's happening in the community will inform decisions you make about programming. You may be successful in establishing new partners in the community with businesses, youth centers, or schools, and you might utilize existing community events to develop programming opportunities, such as having storytime at a farmer's market. By learning about the community and developing new relationships, you have countless opportunities to fill in huge gaps and develop new interests.

Once you complete your assessment, discover gaps, and create a plan that includes goals for new programs, you are ready to search for and develop new programming. As they say, imitation is the highest form of flattery, but before you can imitate another library's successful programs, you need to talk with fellow librarians about what programs are working for them and capture the nuances of their success. If you have the opportunity, you can also explore webinars or workshops that showcase exciting programs. Still, one of the simplest ways to discover fun programs is to search online for successful programs in your region, in the state, and across the country. Searching libraries for program offerings online will inspire new possibilities for your library and may serve as a springboard to enhance existing programs.

Since it's always good to share our own successes, the following programs were ones that I successfully held at my library, and hopefully, these ideas will inspire you.

- Baby Yoga—After training and obtaining my baby yoga certification from ChildLight Yoga in Dover, New Hampshire, I offered six-week sessions for babies and their caregivers. Each set of participants had a mat to sit on and a soft pillow for their baby. Calming music was played as I did various baby yoga poses with a very realistic baby doll that caregivers would imitate with their own babies. Recently, a parent caught my eye and asked if I was the librarian who had done the Baby Yoga program offered several years ago. When I confirmed it, she conveyed her gratitude for the opportunity to bond even more closely with her baby and to take much-needed time to relax and rest. Her words reminded me how touching and beautiful the program was, especially for new parents and caregivers.
- Harry Potter Club—As HP appeals to all ages, it was important to emphasize that all ages were welcome at this very successful program. Most kids would show up to the club dressed as a Harry Potter character, and we'd do HP-themed crafts, have an HP-themed snack, read from sections of one of the books, and, if time allowed or it was planned, watch a movie. It was in this program that kids memorized and performed the "Harry Potter in 99 Seconds" song mentioned at the beginning of this chapter. Beginning each meeting with "current events" was a fun way to find out if kids had seen the latest HP film released, or which book they were reading or had just finished. A favorite moment occurred when a young fourth grader announced he had just finished the second book in the series. The rest of the group erupted in unsolicited, spontaneous applause; this is a moment that has stayed with me!
- Crazy 8s Math Club—I can't say enough about this program for grades K–5. Even if you struggle with numbers (and I do), this program is fun, informative, and gets kids comfortable with math concepts. Best of all, especially for those on shoestring budgets, it's nearly free. The Bedtime Math folks created this series of recreational after-school math programs and activities to help kids find the fun in math. I truly wish I had had this program offered when I was a child; numbers still terrify me. The Crazy 8s Math Club website states that "Crazy 8s is the nation's largest recreational math club for kids in grades K–5. Since 2014, we've served 200,000 kids with 30,000 kits donated to 14,000 coaches in 10,000 locations."[27] Crazy 8s Math sends kits that include almost everything you need to see the program through. Note that there are adherences to honor after setting up an account that includes a ten-minute live call with Crazy 8s folks who

outline the program and answer questions. Again, this program was always full and had a wait list. I never knew math activities and games could be so much fun! All activities offered include a step-by-step guide to implement the activities. Kids loved getting to do all kinds of fun activities, which often seemed more like games, including, at one time, testing volume by yelling at the top of their lungs. Suffice it to say they were thrilled to be screaming in the library! Other popular activities included games played on giant floor mats, learning about colors by mixing colored clay, and building little airplanes with functioning lights and then racing them to learn about distance. Crazy 8s opened my eyes and the eyes of all the participants to realize that math was so much more than numbers as we played with patterns, lengths, and other measurements.

- Lego Club and the Lego Harry Potter Hogwarts Castle—This program grew out of luck and then quite a bit of money. I happened to mention to just the right parent that I was looking for Legos to start a Lego club; you may find it hard to believe (I still do) that she literally walked out of the library, went to her car, and returned with no fewer than three huge garbage bags full of Legos. She confessed that she carried various things around and distributed them where they were needed. Thus, the Lego Club was born. I held the program weekly and often included a building challenge, but kids really loved just having time for free play. Structures built were put on display for library patrons to see, and occasionally, a prize of a new smaller Lego set was offered to the most inventive creation. This led to my obsession with the Lego Harry Potter Hogwarts Castle. I need to clarify that while it was initially my obsession, kids were soon interested. I solicited funds from the Friends of the Library, and without blinking, they provided the nearly $500 dollars it cost to purchase. Building ensued weekly and involved caregivers and kids. It was, of course, displayed proudly for all to see. You can find the castle online at the Lego store if you wish to make a big purchase!

- May the 4th Be with You—I had an overpacked house for this fun Star Wars event held on, obviously, May the 4th. My team and I created a Star Wars passport to be stamped at the many stations set up with fun activities and included Star Wars-themed snacks. A visit from a few of the 501st Legion of Stormtroopers rounded out the day, along with a surprise visit from Darth Vader. It may surprise those who do not follow the series closely but the Stormtroopers can be called upon through various Garrisons set up around the country. In my area, the group offered their presence at no cost. Checking around the country, I see there's a robust Garrison in California called the Southern California Garrison, whose motto is "Bad Guys Doing Good."[28]

- Lock-Ins with Teen Advisory Boards—Use your best judgment, but the teens I had on my advisory board were incredible. I'd hold these overnight "lock-ins" on Saturday beginning at 3:00 when the library closed, and since the library was closed on Sunday, it permitted a leisurely wake-up time with breakfast, and I had plenty of time to clean up after folks went home. I had a full house for **Every. Single. Lock-In**. I planned all sorts of activities, and one time, when *Hamilton* was most popular, kids pretty much spent the night singing the songs. No matter what I planned, though, their favorite activity, one they could do all night and into the wee hours of the morning, was to play hide-and-seek throughout the two floors of the library. To this day, I smile as I recall some of the most unique and clever places kids hid. A former teen advisory board member who is currently a college student returned to work as a page at the library recently and mentioned how much she loved those overnights. We laughed about how a nearly six-foot-tall kid could fit into a cupboard under the coffee maker. I still don't get how he managed that. It was at this program that I began the Midnight Walking Tacos mentioned at the start of this chapter—a huge hit. This is clearly a teen program, but it could work for middle schoolers as well. Additionally, as a prize for summer reading, I've seen younger children stay at the library overnight with their families.

- Movie Marathons—After the summer reading program concluded but before school started again, I offered three-day movie marathons. This was outrageously successful as the community meeting room was nearly filled. I invited kids to bring sleeping bags, pillows, and lunch; the library provided pizza dinner, and we'd watch movies most of the day. The most successful marathon, not surprisingly, was the Harry Potter Movie Marathon. Kids were encouraged to dress up, to act out scenes while the film was playing, to do an activity or exercise every time a movie character said certain words, and I'd always bring out a trolley loaded with treats seen in the films, including acid pops and chocolate frogs, when the Hogwarts students were on the train heading to school and yelled out "Anything from the Trolley?" If you're familiar with the participatory nature of *The Rocky Horror Picture Show*, you'll understand the interactive nature of this program. I have to share a moving moment I had every time I featured a particular HP film: When the characters in the film held up their wands to signify the passing of a key and beloved character, the kids in the library, unprompted, got up and did the same; I had tears streaming every time.
- Beading—This community partnership was immensely successful. A local bead shop owner taught beaded bracelet patterns to a few librarians for free—in turn, we paid for the cost of discounted materials. Later, I would teach young patrons how to make these creations after purchasing supplies from the bead store, again at a discount, with funds from the Friends of the Library. Additionally, if kids showed up at the bead store, they merely had to mention the library program and received discounts. The shop owner wins, the kids win by learning a new beaded pattern, and the librar-

ian and library win by offering a fun program. The wait list to participate in the program was a thing.

Please note that these programs are merely representative of what might be offered in a library; librarians must assess their value according to their community's needs.

THE BENEFITS OF PROGRAMMING IN MULTIPLE FORMATS

In this section, there is a bit of reinforcement of the previously mentioned concept that when you're planning programs, consider not only developmentally appropriate activities, but also consider appealing to a wide range of interests in the community; when this is considered, the library is valued beyond providing books and other physical materials, and the community exacts direct benefits as well. Perhaps best articulated through the National Impact of Library Public Programs Assessment (NILPPA), the benefits to public library programming are threefold: individuals, the community, and the library itself benefit from offering diverse programming options, and here's how, as seen on their site:

- Individuals will benefit: Library programs are opportunities for continuing education and lifelong learning. They serve residents of all ages and income levels. They serve a community's diversity through engaging entertainment, enrichment, and opportunities to encounter new ideas and learn new skills.
- Communities will benefit: Programming helps develop a community voice and can support civic dialogues. It helps foster community networks, introduces residents, invites newcomers, and allows exploration of ideas in a safe environment. Programming opens doors to new partnerships that can extend the community identity.
- Libraries will benefit: Cultural programs build awareness of the library and its value within the community, drawing increased attention to many important services the library provides. Program audiences are likely to return to the library to use collections and access electronic resources. They are also likely to communicate the value of the library to others.[29]

To wrap up this section, children's services, and particularly programming, according to Adele Fasick and Leslie Edmonds Holt, fall into three areas—marketing, enrichment, and reading enhancement programs.[30] Marketing the library, as I've mentioned, is not the primary goal in program planning, but the library benefits nonetheless; keeping the library relevant in the community and ensuring visibility is important, so programming, especially when advertised properly, will provide the community with buy-in, helping community members recognize the value of the library. As an example, years ago, I applied for and received a grant to purchase iPads for use in a program for elderly patrons at a nearby nursing home. Young patrons from the teen advisory board met with the seniors and taught them to use the iPads to connect with their families. This program was successful, and a newspaper article helped the community realize that the library offers more than just books and movies.

Enrichment and enhancement programs, simply put, provide participants with opportunities by enriching participants' library experience on a variety of levels through education, engagement, and learning programs. Common examples, according to Fasick and Holt, include makerspace programs for self-discovery, book clubs, and craft and activity programs that tie to the library's collection.[31] As with all programming, it's important to remember to tie the programming to literacy, the collection, and especially, as mentioned previously, to the library's mission and vision statements.

VIRTUAL PROGRAMS

In 2019, library program offerings shifted seismically due to the worldwide Covid-19 pandemic. During the period of shutdown in which many libraries closed their doors to the public, librarians sought to find ways to continue programming. This required creativity, and the online program was born. Thanks to the proliferation of Zoom, reaching the community could still occur despite fears around the contagion. Years later, in 2023 as I write this, virtual programming is alive and well despite lower transmission rates; just last night (January 26, 2023), I attended a remarkable storytelling event entitled "Winter Tales with Anne Jennison." Anne shared several Abenaki/Wabanaki tales that captivated audience members. The format worked beautifully, and attendance was good. Benefits of hosting online events include the eventual recording posted for even more patrons to access, and any issues with weather are avoided, so the program will go on.

There are tips and tricks for successful online programming, not to mention legal issues that must be considered. Rebecca Ogle has written an excellent book, *Virtual Storytimes*,[32] and this resource may be applied not only to storytimes but to other online programming as well. In addition to this excellent text, seek out the expertise of the ALA's "Virtual Storytimes Services Guide." At this site, you'll discover technology and copyright information, promotion tips, and program ideas, among other offerings. They even solicit feedback and creative ideas that may be submitted to the site, making this a wonderfully collaborative and valuable resource for librarians offering online programs.

Like in-person programming, planning for a virtual program begins with considering the audience's needs. Initially, I found it challenging to determine what was most wanted or needed in the community as everyone was dealing with the pandemic in different ways, but I understood early on that storytime was an important program to continue offering during this strange time.

Once the virtual program is planned, I recommend requiring registration to avoid potential disruptive intrusions, known as "Zoombombing." Patrons simply sign up to attend a program and provide their email address; links are then sent to those in attendance along with a password. Attendees enter a waiting area, and the library checks the name against registrations before moving participants into the synchronous session. These are all settings available in most Zoom accounts. Check with your library to determine the type of account you have and adjust as needed.

Storytime seemed to be where most libraries began their online offerings. From there, librarians explored what was being offered at other libraries or created new and exciting programs to meet community needs. Included in library programs during this difficult time, one creative concept explored was Reader's Theatre using Shakespeare's *A Midsummer Night's Dream*; character parts were assigned and recorded, then blended to create a coherent play. A fun collaboration, the result wasn't bad and was often quite funny. So many other creative online programs are out there. Do not miss exploring Pinterest! Folks have chimed in with a multitude of creative ideas from virtual escape rooms to bad art nights and how to offer virtual STEM—a wonderful resource for ideas.[33]

In-person storytimes engage children in many ways and transferring that to a virtual storytime presents challenges. Encouraging children to keep their video feed open will help the librarian to connect better with the kids during synchronous programs. Rather than engage children in synchronous storytime, many libraries offered pre-recorded or asynchronous storytimes for viewing.

In whatever way you approach virtual programming for children, be sure to research carefully to determine the best format, and keeping a positive outlook is helpful. You may be encouraged by Ogle's perspective: "I, somehow, miraculously, am not tired of virtual storytime. I feel invigorated by what the tech and business worlds refer to as disruption."[34] Sounds like a good way to approach what seems to be a continuance of necessary online programming.

Programming in the library is an opportunity to offer rich and varied experiences for library patrons that benefit individuals, the library, and the community. By aligning offerings with the library's mission statement, vision statement, and strategic plan, and by properly evaluating programming impact, the library becomes not just a brick-and-mortar structure of books but also a thriving community center. With storytime as a foundation, the library will serve all manner of families and ensure the development of lifelong learners.

REVIEW QUESTIONS

1. Outline the basic steps of storytime and why each element is considered important.

2. What is the concept of emergent literacy, and why is it important to consider when preparing storytime for babies?
3. When planning programming, what is the most important foundation necessary for success?
4. Outline the various age levels of library storytime participants and discuss how the structure for storytime might be different for each age group.
5. What is the challenge of family storytime?
6. Articulate your thoughts around the necessity of including conversations about race in storytimes.
7. Explore your library—either one where you work or your town, city, or county branch. Seek out virtual programming and assess what is being offered.

NOTES

1. Katie Fitzgerald, *Story Time Success: A Practical Guide for Librarians* (Lanham, MD: Rowman & Littlefield, 2016), 1.
2. Megan Dowd Lambert, *Reading Picture Books with Children: How to Shake Up Storytime and Get Kids Talking About What They See* (Watertown, MA: Charlesbridge, 2015), vii.
3. Ibid., x.
4. Ibid., x.
5. Ibid., vii–xii.
6. Saroj Nadkarni Ghoting and Kathy Fling Klatt, *STEP Into Storytime: Using StoryTime Effective Practice to Strengthen the Development of Newborns to Five-Year-Olds* (Chicago: ALA Editions, 2014), 19.
7. American Library Association—ALA Member News, "ALSC Names Betsy Diamant-Cohen as 2022 Distinguished Service Award Winner," accessed January 12, 2023, https://www.ala.org/news/member-news/2022/03/alsc-names-betsy-diamant-cohen-2022-distinguished-service-award-winner.
8. Mother Goose on the Loose, "The Basic MGOL Program," accessed January 12, 2023, https://mgol.net/the-basic-mgol-program/.
9. Betsy Diamant-Cohen, *Mother Goose on the Loose: A Handbook and CD-ROM Kit with Scripts, Rhymes, Songs, Flannel-Board Patterns, and Activities for Promoting Early Childhood Development* (New York: Neal-Schuman Publishers, Inc., 2006), xi.
10. Ibid., 3.
11. Ibid., 3.
12. Betsy Diamant-Cohen, *Mother Goose on the Loose: Updated!* (Chicago: ALA Editions, 2019), 16.
13. Ibid.
14. Ibid.
15. Ibid., 17.
16. Ibid., 17.
17. Ibid., 17–18.

18. MCLSKIDS—"Storytime Names," accessed January 14, 2023, http://mclskids.pbworks.com/w/page/25069678/Storytime%20Names.
19. Kate, [Instant Messenger] Lisa Houde, January 13, 2023, Instant Messenger feed.
20. Wikipedia, "Drag Queen Story Hour," accessed January 28, 2023, https://en.wikipedia.org/wiki/Drag_Queen_Story_Hour.
21. Drag Story Hour, "Mission," accessed January 28, 2023, https://www.dragstoryhour.org/.
22. Ibid.
23. Lee Brown, "Protestors Clash Outside Drag Story Hour at Queens Library," accessed January 28, 2023, from https://nypost.com/2022/12/29/protesters-clash-outside-drag-story-hour-at-nyc-library/.
24. Katie Gillespie, "At Drag Queen Story Hour, Children 'just see the love,'" accessed January 28, 2023, https://www.columbian.com/news/2019/oct/28/at-drag-queen-story-hour-children-just-see-the-love/.
25. Whimsy Librarian, "Let's Talk About Race Workshop Series—Overview," accessed January 28, 2023, http://whimsylibrarian.com/lets-talk-about-race-workshop-series.
26. Lindsey Krabbenhoft, "Guest Post: Talking to Kids About Race in Storytime and The Let's Talk About Race Toolkit," accessed January 28, 2023, https://jbrary.com/guest-post-talking-to-kids-about-race-in-storytime-and-the-lets-talk-about-race-tooklkit/.
27. Crazy 8s Club, "Nothing like your usual math club," accessed January 15, 2023 https://crazy8sclub.org/.
28. Southern California Garrison, "Welcome to the 501st Legion Southern California Garrison," accessed January 15, 2023, http://southerncaliforniagarrison.com/home/.
29. National Impact of Library Public Programs Assessment, "NILPPA's Role in Understanding the Importance of Public Programming," accessed January 27, 2023, https://nilppa.org/phase-1-white-paper/nilppas-role-in-understanding-the-importance-of-public-programming/.
30. Adele M. Fasick and Leslie Edmonds Holt, *Managing Children's Services in Libraries, 4th Edition* (Santa Barbara, CA: Libraries Unlimited, 2013), 124.
31. Ibid., 130.
32. Rebecca Ogle, *Virtual Storytimes: A Practical Guide for Librarians* (Lanham, MD: Rowman & Littlefield, 2022).
33. Pinterest, Angela Parker, "Library-Virtual Programming," accessed January 27, 2023, https://www.pinterest.com/texasdogmom/library-virtual-programming/.
34. Ogle, *Virtual Storytimes*, xi.

4

The Summer Reading Program

Everything about the summer reading program (SRP) just spells out FUN! Sunny weather, lazy afternoons reading in a tree or hammock, attending animal programs at the library—it's all part of the excitement. As a young person, I remember my own carefree hot summer days riding my bike, lounging with a book, or just hanging out with my friends. The summer reading program, while fun, is much more than that. A well-constructed summer reading program, one that partners with the local schools, will help prevent a phenomenon known as the "summer slide." Summer reading is a kind of educational opportunity disguised as fun. In this chapter, I'll explain why summer reading is so important and will provide organizational tips and tricks and all you need to hold an effective and exciting summer reading program.

WHY CREATE AND IMPLEMENT A SUMMER READING PROGRAM?

The library's SRP will help you grow and become resourceful, organized, and recognized in the community as you create, promote, and implement a fabulous SRP. Before guiding you on this exciting SRP journey, let's first answer a question: Why is this important? There are many reasons, and among them are preventing the dreaded summer slide, engaging children with books and reading, building relationships with multiple stakeholders, and ensuring your children's department is vibrant and holds a place in the minds and hearts of community residents.

SUMMER SLIDE / SUMMER LEARNING LOSS

The term "summer slide" is a well-documented and researched phenomenon. Children need continuity in education, and when the school term ends and summer begins, that continuity is disrupted. Thus, the need for the library's summer reading program is critical. While the term was new to me as a first-time teacher, it has been around for over one hundred years. According to David Quinn and Morgan Polikoff, "This phenomenon—sometimes referred to as summer learning loss, summer setback, or summer slide—has been of interest to education researchers going back as far as 1906."[1] Understanding what summer slide is isn't complicated; it's pretty much what it sounds like—learning loss over the summer, but this is the definition according to the U.S. Department of Education: "Summer is the perfect time for students of all ages to relax, but it's also a time when summer learning loss can occur. This learning loss is called the 'summer slide,' and happens when children do not engage in educational activities during the summer months."[2] Interestingly, the Colorado Department of Education further explains how the term is defined with a bit more nuance: "'Summer slide' is the tendency for students, especially those from low-income families, to lose some of the achievement gains they made during the previous school year."[3] Clearly, the need for a summer reading program is critical to continuous development, but research shows different ages are not impacted by the learning loss in the same way. According to Quinn and Polikoff,

> The authors concluded that: (1) on average, students' achievement scores declined over summer vacation by one month's worth of school-year learning, (2) declines were sharper for math than for reading, and (3) the extent of loss was larger at higher grade levels. Importantly, they also concluded that income-based reading gaps grew over the summer, given that middle class students tended to show improvement in reading skills while lower-income students tended to experience loss. However, they did not find differential summer learning in math, or by gender or race in either subject.[4]

What stands out to me about these findings is that there is more achievement loss at higher grade levels than younger. It's a bit tricky to keep students engaged in the library as they grow older, but collaborating with middle or high school teachers will ensure that these groups will be successful. Additionally, income levels impact student success, so careful planning will help the library prepare a program for everyone.

Did you notice the inclusion of math in the learning loss report? I've seen libraries include math challenges as part of the summer reading program to great effect. What might you consider doing to keep kids from the "summer math slide?"

ORGANIZATION AND PLANNING: THE KEY TO SUCCESS

First, you need to plan, and you need to begin your planning early. Ideally, you'll want to start during the winter months as your SRP is right around the corner, typically beginning in June and ending in August—though that varies regionally. Besides, if you're in a colder winter climate as I am, just thinking about summer in the winter can make the cold more bearable, right? You'll also want to get organized, so grab your new summer reading notebook or create a new file and begin with RESOURCES. I love a list, and we'll be making many; plus, they help you get organized and keep you from getting overwhelmed.

FUNDING RESOURCES

Your first subcategory under resources, you may guess, is funding. What sort of funds do you have from your general budget? Talk with your supervisor or the head of youth services to find out what funding has been set aside, if any. If you look at the bottom line and find it lacking, don't worry, list your other potential funding sources, for example, the library's Friends of the Library groups. There may also be grants available that can be found with simple Google searches. Funding will pay for performers, prizes, outreach materials, theme décor, and hospitality, such as pizza dinners, snacks at programs, and edible incentives. In some libraries, specific funding may also be required to purchase books that correlate with the SRP theme. Again, if your funding is sparse, look to your next resource, community partners.

Your library may have established relationships with local businesses, other town departments such as the Recreation and Emergency Management departments, local schools, and possibly other children's organizations in your community. If not, developing relationships is very important, and it may mean that you will need to stretch your comfort zone by actively going out and meeting with business owners and others. Each one of these groups can play a critical role in the success of your summer reading program. Your community partners may help you with food, outreach, funding, prizes, and venues, so make sure you identify those important potential partners. As an example, in my small community of Rye, one of our local restaurants is also one of my favorite summertime stops for ice cream. That small eatery has provided our summer reading program with several vats of ice cream for our pet show-off and ice cream social event—and they've donated that ice cream at no charge. Pets and ice cream are a big draw, and this pet show-off is a showcase of what kids love about their pets—so endearing! This is always a well-attended event because, really, who doesn't love a free ice cream sundae on a hot summer evening? Hey, come back! Stop right there; no running to the fridge for ice cream now; we need to get back to our lists!

One more note about the generosity of local businesses and the Friends group; it's critical to acknowledge those groups with a thank-you note. Thanking the funder and including some anecdotes that show how their donations made a difference will go a long way to future relationships with those businesses and Friends groups. People love to hear stories about how the kids enjoyed their library program, and your sponsors are no different.

TO THEME OR NOT TO THEME?

Next, consider whether you'll include a theme or perhaps skip a theme altogether. In my experiences, themes are fantastic and help focus the aesthetics, slogans, and even book selections for your displays. Will you follow your state's theme? They likely have one, or you may want to go rogue and create your own. When thinking about this, consider what has been traditionally done in your library and what expectations children may have. It's easy to determine whether your state has its own theme by conducting a simple Google search.

Long ago, the children's librarians in New Hampshire created elaborate summer themes from scratch; they hired a local illustrator, met to create programming ideas, and chose book titles and all the elements that comprise an SRP theme. I remember well the meeting in which the vote took place to either abandon the creative individual process or adopt the nationwide Collaborative Summer Library Program (CSLP). The vote went with the national program, and New Hampshire has followed that format since. Massachusetts also follows an established program by utilizing iREAD. You may opt to, as I mentioned, go rogue and do your own thing! I tried that one summer, and while it was a lot of fun, it was also a lot of work. I quickly jumped back into the CSLP offerings, and you'll find the resources within those programs to be nothing short of phenomenal. Before downloadable options existed, the New Hampshire State Library took orders for physical binders from all state libraries who wanted to participate in the CSLP theme and would distribute them on the state's interlibrary loan van routes; every year, I counted on that notebook and was thrilled when it arrived.

For 2024, CSLP's theme is "Adventure Begins at Your Library," and iREAD's is "Read, Renew, and Repeat." There are many useful materials and resources available to you if your library follows one of these programs. Head to the CSLP website to view the offerings at https://www.cslpreads.org/. Membership at the CSLP is required for access to all materials, but non-members may view some of what's offered. Typically, the state library subscribes and provides access information to libraries; however, if your state does not subscribe and you'd like to use the CSLP, the cost for an annual membership is, get this, only $20. So affordable.

But why use the CLSP? According to their site, "The Collaborative Summer Library Program (CSLP) is a 501(c)3 non-profit organization that exists to make summer programming meaningful and accessible to all library patrons. We provide the tools and resources needed to make running a summer program affordable and successful for all participating libraries."[5] I couldn't agree more! This nonprofit clearly takes their work seriously and works hard to create meaningful resources; their ideas are so much fun! Among the best things about the CSLP is this: "CSLP is committed to providing resources, materials, and opportunities that reflect the diversity of our communities including all races, ethnicities, national origins, genders, and all other identities."[6] Among their resources, you'll find images, advertisement flyers, programs with specific resources to complete those programs, videos explaining how to complete the activities—and so much more. While I have experience with this program, other offerings will provide similar materials and resources; you have only to search to determine what is out there and what will work for your community.

On the other hand, if you do want to create your own program, you'll need a process to determine its theme. Enlist the help of an existing student group, create a patron or staff poll, and establish an SRP committee, but do coordinate with your local school. Back to your notebook: Once you've determined your theme, explore and list available resources to see what fits for your library.

PLANNING DATES AND TIMES

Add a calendar to your notebook (or file) and start filling in dates. When will the summer reading program begin, and when will it end? A key factor to help you determine these dates is learning when your local elementary school closes for the summer. You have about eight weeks between the end of June and mid-August, generally, to fit in everything, so determining the bookends is important. Another possible factor in determining your dates, especially for smaller libraries, is establishing staff coverage. Find out early when staff will be taking vacations, but typically, librarians avoid vacations or time away during the summer. Still, life is life, so make your plans around staff.

Related to the calendar and on your to-do list is the important task of introducing the topic to teachers at local schools. You want to establish dates for classroom visits so that you can get kids excited about the library's summer reading program. Even if you haven't figured everything out at this point, get on their calendar early. Coordinate with teachers' best times, typically in late May to early June. I often visited during the last week of school as I had extensive packets of information for parents and caregivers and would hand them out then—there was less of a chance that kids would lose them as it's so close to the end of the school year!

Next on the calendar, I was lucky enough to attend a state library-sponsored performer showcase, so if that opportunity is available to you, be sure to note the date and attend! More on this later. Knowing your budget and calendar, you should book performers early, especially for the all-important SRP kick-off event and finale.

I've typically held SRPs for six weeks, and I waited a week between the last day of school and the library's kick-off event. While this worked in my community, it may not in yours. After the six weeks, three weeks remained between the finale of the SRP and the start of school. Again, in my community, this was when families typically took longer vacations, but this may not be the experience in other communities. You'll need to determine what works best for your community. With that said, after the SRP was officially over, I held programs during those three weeks that always included a movie marathon event that I mentioned in chapter 3.

ASSESSING YOUR VENUES AND CONSIDERING SPACE NEEDS

You have your theme, you've started your calendar, you've established community partners, and you have a good idea about the budget; next, you need to think about venues. You need to consider space in the library if you share that space with other departments. Your library patrons' space needs may have changed since Covid. Some families may be reluctant to attend a crowded indoor event, especially if they have a vulnerable member of the family—or perhaps this is no longer a concern in your community. Get your notebook out again and list venue possibilities for both indoor and outdoor options.

You'll want to include on your list an estimate of how many people each location can hold. Also, you'll want to know if there is seating/space available for people of all ages and abilities, stroller space for caregivers with babies, and wheelchair accessibility. If your library has an accessible outdoor venue, that's great; if not, evaluate community partners to identify any spaces they may have to share. This may be a nearby park, a local school gym, or a local business. For these venues, you'll need to consider their accessibility by walking, bicycling, car, and transit. Is there enough parking? Are there any amenities, like bathrooms, water, or shade? Are the locations centrally located or well-known and used among residents? Does the library have a good relationship with the property owner or caretaker? If it's a great space, consider expanding your relationships and reach out to find out if there's any interest in collaborating with the library. Whether outdoor or indoor, list all the limitations and advantages of each space, especially availability, then continue your planning. Also, if you know your event will draw bigger numbers than your library can accommodate, consider booking a school gym or perhaps utilizing an open-air venue such as a park. If you have a limited budget, you will likely not want to pay for a venue, so make sure it's no cost to the library. Now you see why a planning notebook is needed!

HIRING PERFORMERS

Isn't this great? Your summer reading program is coming together with its theme, schedule, program budget, staffing, and venue availability. Still, you may be wondering about which acts to hire and how many paid performers you can arrange. Work with your library staff and find out what the local favorites have been in the past and inquire about repeat performers or find new acts. Next, check your state library's resources. You might also get in touch with local librarians to see what's been successful at their libraries. I had great success teaming up with other libraries to share travel costs; occasionally, if two libraries booked on the same day, even more discounts were available.

With your budget in mind, divide your summer reading program into segments: you'll want a fun, crowd-drawing opener, a festive midway celebration, and a spectacular finale as highlights; this was the structure I employed knowing that the Friends of the Library would be sponsoring at least three programs. An important note here—when you introduce your program, always give a nod of appreciation to the sponsor, and include that in your advertising on social media and flyers.

Knowing your budget and the timeframes, list possible acts and start calling to find out who is available and when they are available. Book as early as you can; over time, you'll get familiar with the performers and can get those programs booked well in advance. In your conversation with performers, be sure to share your SRP theme so they may incorporate it in their presentations when possible. Most performers find a way to do this beautifully.

What to do if you don't have a budget for performers? Ask around and look to volunteers, town and library staff, and library patrons. Get the word out about what you are looking for and partner with local agencies or other town departments. They may be willing to share and partner with you—perhaps you could partner with a recreation or parks department for a music event.

Performer showcases are another option if this is available in your community, region, or state. I loved it when, prior to the Covid-19 pandemic, the state library of New Hampshire held an annual performer showcase. Librarians from around the state attended and were treated as if we were the kids in the audience attending the program! We'd sing, jump around, get up on stage as volunteers—it was an absolute blast! It was a great way to assess a possible performer as a fit for the community. I hired so many exciting performers for the summer reading program from attending this event. Perhaps this is something offered through your state library; it's worth checking.

If I were pressed to share the most popular programs I held, it would always be the magicians! Kids cannot get enough of a magic act, and after the program, books on how to do magic flew off the shelves! The best performers are those who interact with kids and get them up dancing or participating in some way, and I had several magicians who befuddled kids with their tricks and included them in the show. The other extremely popular events were those which included live animals. A local wildlife rescue organization, Wildlife Encounters, regularly provided incredible entertainment and education for kids. The kids couldn't get enough of petting snakes like a Burmese Python and "Tudor," the 100-plus-pound Giant Sulcata Tortoise, or getting a close-up view of animals like "Savannah," a Bennett's Wallaby; "Isis," an African Serval Cat; "Domino," an Adult African Crested Porcupine; and "Ivan," a Turkey Vulture.[7] This was one event I had to hold at the school gymnasium due to the huge crowd.

PROGRAM CREATION

Aside from your performers, you will want to create a variety of theme-related programs to fill out your calendar that encourage your young patrons to participate. Foundational to the summer reading program is to encourage reading. Creating themed displays of a variety of materials is your bread and butter of the SRP. Naturally, you want to appeal to different age groups and different interests. Creating unique displays that include a variety of books and materials that appeal to various age groups, including fiction, nonfiction, graphic novels, and children's picture books, is key. Remember, kids want to see themselves in the materials, so make sure your choices are diverse.

In organizing your library programs, consider engaging existing library clubs or youth groups in the community that might sponsor a poetry jam, a local author book talk, or a music event. Hosting an outdoor pet show in which every pet wins a ribbon is always fun. You'll want to review any funding needs for these programs, such as food, prizes, outreach materials, and so on, and look again to your budget and community partners to help with those needs. These family-friendly events ensure everyone in the family can join in on the fun. Each event is another opportunity for you to provide more outreach about your SRP offerings.

Not everyone wants to read a dozen books or more over the summer, so establishing games and activities related to the summer theme are great ways to create more engaging experiences to encourage more reading. Guessing jars are a tried-and-true technique, and they can be filled with all manner of things: candy, marbles, plastic bugs, small balls, or toys. Consider the theme and let your imagination run wild. Scavenger hunts are a great way to engage young patrons to find items related to your summer theme. If placed strategically, a scavenger hunt will also ensure participants become aware of various sections in the stacks around the children's library. All that is needed are small cards with clues, and once each item is checked off, the participant can trade the card in for "library bucks" or a prize. Creating themed mazes, word puzzles, and coloring pages are also ways to engage a non-reader. Daily or weekly trivia was a staple in the summer reading program, and kids rushed in to answer a question and earn a library buck. Wondering about library bucks, aren't you? I'll get to that in the promotion section.

Aside from the self-guided or passive program activities, make-and-take craft kits related to the summer theme are always fun for kids. You may even encourage participants to make the kits at the library or to take them home and bring them back to the library to display the finished craft. This will accomplish several things: it will be an advertisement of the activity; it may become part of the theme décor; but most importantly, participants will return to the library for another visit. Don't underestimate the value of passive programming; some kids prefer the ease of this low-key activity over the excitement of a large, noisy performer program.

PROMOTION/PUBLICITY/OUTREACH

You've done all the prep work and made all the arrangements with performers and venues, but now you must get people involved, coming into the library, participating in programs, and, of course, reading. You'll want to develop multiple strategies to highlight your theme and develop outreach materials. Keep in mind, when creating outreach materials such as posters, handouts, emails, and postcards, it's important to use the byline and any logo that may accompany the theme. Next, cover all the usual bases: create email blasts, post on social media, and update the library's website. Write brief press releases for the local newspaper or, for rural communities, the local newsletter. Post on the library's website calendar all the scheduled events, the featured performers, the locations, and the dates and times in all advertisement material. Also, remember to acknowledge any partnering businesses or funders and include artwork or slogans of your summer reading program theme; this bears repeating!

As I mentioned earlier, one of the first outreach elements is the school visit. This means you've reached out to the school or to specific teachers and planned to talk with students. Bring your "A" game, be enthusiastic, and show excitement about the theme, the programs, prizes, and all those things you've arranged. Have giveaways and handouts like postcards that highlight where students and their caregivers might find more details on the library's website; this is one option, but I mentioned the annual SRP folder that I created. Contents of the folder (purchased with the annual theme's artwork) included a recommended reading list for the ages of each of the classes, a welcome letter to caregivers enumerating the many reasons the SRP is important, highlights of scheduled events, an SRP calendar, a coloring sheet related to the theme, a bookmark purchased with theme-related artwork, theme-related stickers, a reading log or instructions about how to keep track of how many pages or books were read using an app like *beanstack*, and a color-changing mood pencil stamped with the library's name and contact information. This was so much fun; kids got excited to get their annual packet, and I made sure to hold interactive school visits to really get energy going around the SRP.

READING AND PROGRAM MEASUREMENT OPTIONS: MAKING READING A GOAL

Helping young readers track their progress can be very rewarding. Whether they are tracking their progress by reading one book or multiple books, acknowledging their progress in a notebook with stickers, other visual methods, or online apps can be all the incentive a young reader needs to meet their individual reading goals. Some elements a young reader can track are the number of hours, number of pages, or the number of books they've read. Creating a standard reading log for each participating young patron will encourage their progress. I've also seen great success with massive bulletin boards in which a child has a marker—and these typically align with the summer theme—and each time a goal is met, they move the marker themselves. I love this option because it brings the child back to the library to mark progress and encourages finding that next book; it's also a great representation of their success—visible to all—and that success may encourage another young reader to get his, her, or their own marker going and get reading!

Before leaving the discussion around tracking reading, it's also important to acknowledge participation in non-reading activities. Non-readers may eventually become readers, enjoy audiobooks, or even become interested in visual materials. Whichever it is, encouragement to participate in the library's movies, music venues, games, and other events and activities will build important connections for that young person. Tracking their participation will also ensure that the young person will feel included and successful.

BEANSTACK

I want to include a plug for *beanstack* as this tool is a fun and powerful help in tracking reading; plus, it's a really cool company. Take a few moments to check out their website and their origins here: https://www.beanstack.com/about-us/our-story. The company started when the founders were reading to their two-year-old son, which moved them to creating a business model that got buy-in from Mark Cuban on *Shark Tank*, and eventually, that model developed into the business that it is today.[8] Statistics listed on their site include the participation of 2,500-plus libraries, 6,000-plus school buildings, 180 school districts, and 13.8-plus million readers.[9] Impressive! When our library first utilized this customizable app, I was enthralled and loved cataloging titles, pages, and minutes read. One of my favorite things about *beanstack*, among the many, is the company motto of three words: love, inclusion, and awesomeness. There is a cost for this app, so explore their "get a quote" area to find out if this is right for your library and community. Other reading apps are out there, like READsquared and Accelerated Reader, but I've found *beanstack* to be the best value for the many functions offered.

INCENTIVES: CANDY, COOKIES, AND TOYS—YES, PLEASE!

Picture it: You're in fourth grade, looking out the window of your classroom, the end of school is right around the corner, and since school may not be your favorite place, you are excited to get out and go bike riding and exploring with your friends, sleeping in and playing video games, eating junk food when you can sneak it, and what? Go to the library? How is that going to happen? Prizes, that's how. Incentives work. Not exactly comparable to children, but I have a small poodle, Kiki; she is very smart, loves her treats, and she loves to play. Learning a new command or trick for a treat or some ball playing is all the incentive she needs. Incentives for kids to participate in reading can also be fun and effective. Whether you've received donations or have purchased supplies yourself, creating a library store for young patrons who earn library bucks to spend in the store for reaching their goals is a good incentive. The Friends of the Library are typically generous and may fully fund the incentives, but be sure to involve student volunteers in creating and staffing the store, when possible, as they may remember how much fun they had when cashing in their own well-earned library bucks.

Little prizes are great, but you could also provide raffle tickets for kids that they can place in raffle prize buckets; you might have three bigger prizes each summer to raffle off. Kids love this and look forward to the drawing. I've made this part of the culminating experience by pulling the raffle winners at the SRP finale. Here again, local businesses, along with the Friends of the Library, are a great resource. Reach out to those partners for outright donations or discounted prices.

Another thing about incentives. While I've had great success with including prizes during the summer reading program, there is a strong argument against incentivizing reading. Reading should, as one of my colleagues keenly pointed out, be the prize itself. Despite this, the *School Library Journal* conducted a survey that found that, "Of the 773 public libraries that responded, 97 percent use prizes as incentives to motivate readers in their summer reading program. The process is standard: Log those minutes or count pages read, hit a goal, or read more than others, and win a prize."[10] To combat the guilt I sometimes felt over offering these little prizes, I always offered books I had collected over the year as an option alongside the toys. Surprisingly, kids often opted for a book over a little toy they might play with briefly and then forget about.

PROGRAM EVALUATION

This incredibly important element of the SRP cannot be overlooked. While I'm listing this last, the outcomes of the program must be considered while planning is taking place. I'll refer you back to chapter 2 for a refresher. It's just not enough to utilize quantitative measurements, though that's what many libraries do. Consider options that collect real stories of kids and their caregivers and how they grew or changed over the summer and be sure to plan your evaluations as you are creating programming.

SUMMER READING PROGRAM RESOURCES

You'll likely find many resources on your own, but here are a few to get you started. First, the American Library Association's Summer Reading Program Resources LibGuide is a one-stop shop for everything you need. Visit the site here: https://libguides.ala.org/summer-reading/resources/. Among the offerings listed is the CSLP, among others. The CSLP offers materials in English or Spanish, and they include four specialized programs for all ages: Early Literacy Program, Children's Program, Teen Program, and even an Adult Program; if the entire range of patrons participates in the program, there is a unity that kids notice, and they understand they're part of a bigger event and they belong. Be sure to check out the link to their store to see all the fun incentives you might consider purchasing. I was fortunate to have the funds to purchase shirts with the annual themed artwork for all youth staff (you should see my closet full of T-shirts!), bookmarks and stickers for the end-of-school packets, several large banners with the annual artwork, and even staked outdoor signs I could adjust to announce upcoming programs. The artwork is downloadable, so you can use it in all areas of promotion. One of the programs to note for the 2024 summer program is the thoughtful Bird Watch Quest offering; creators at the CSLP included only birds that were found in all regions of the United States, and a printable journal includes images of the birds along with QR codes to hear the sound they make.[11] Isn't this awesome?

I realize that other summer reading programs like the CSLP may be comparable, but I wanted to share this exciting resource that provided so much success in my summer reading program. Once again, the site to visit is: www.cslpreads.org.

One very popular event in my neck of the woods is the annual New England Collaborative Summer Summit, typically held early in March, in which librarians get together from the region to explore new possibilities while examining traditional library offerings. This event is not only entertaining but also practical in that it provides participants with a full-bodied series of resources that will include favorite performers. Once you determine your performers, detail their booking requirements, contact information, and fee structures and reserve them as soon as possible.

Demco offers some great ideas as well at their *33 Winning Summer Reading Program Ideas* site. These include *Partner Up with Hometown Heroes, Focus on All the Literacies, Go to the Movies, Go Camping,* or *Have a Sleepover,* among others.[12]

What you can create for your summer reading program is limitless and bound only by your imagination. By exploring what other libraries might include, you can get your own ideas and alter them to fit your community. I've seen kids running into the program to do the weekly trivia, or jumping up and down when they won the guessing jar, or squealing with absolute delight when they won a raffle prize. But the most heartwarming gift I experienced as a librarian was having kids tell me all about the *BEST* book they'd ever read during the summer.

REVIEW QUESTIONS

1. As you read through this chapter, create your own checklist of steps for summer reading.
2. Outline the concept of "summer slide" and conduct further research. Reflect on your findings.
3. If you work in the library and have created an SRP, report on what works best and other tools you've learned. If you're not yet working in a library, visit your local town or city library branch and conduct an interview with a librarian who works on the program; outline in your reflection details around their successes and tips on things to avoid.
4. What are your thoughts about reading incentives? Outline your reasoning after conducting further research.
5. Explore the CSLP site, and then look into the many offerings listed on the American Library Association's LibGuide; compare and contrast your findings.
6. Have you used *beanstack* or another reading tracker? Explore various alternatives to *beanstack* and compare their offerings to determine which would best meet the needs of your community—whether you're currently working in a library or not.
7. Choose one of the thirty-three Demco ideas not mentioned in this chapter to explore; what resonates with you? Is it something you could implement in your library? If you're not working in a library, focus on what resonates with you and your estimation of what might be effective in the community where you live.

NOTES

1. David M. Quinn and Morgan Polikoff, *Summer Learning Loss: What Is It, and What Can We Do About It?*, accessed February 10, 2024, https://www.brookings.edu/articles/summer-learning-loss-what-is-it-and-what-can-we-do-about-it/.
2. U.S. Department of Education, *Stopping the Summer Slide*, accessed February 10, 2024, https://www.ed.gov/content/stopping-summer-slide.
3. Colorado Department of Education, "Summer Slide and the Importance of Reading Over the Summer," accessed February 10, 2024, https://www.cde.state.co.us/cdelib/summerslide.
4. Quinn and Polikoff, *Summer Learning Loss*.
5. Collaborative Summer Library Program, *Why CSLP?*, accessed February 10, 2024, https://www.cslpreads.org/why-cslp/.
6. Ibid.

7. Wildlife Encounter Ecology and Wellness Center, *About Us*, accessed February 12, 2024, https://www.weecocenter.com/about-us/#aboutanimals.
8. beanstack, *Who We Are*, accessed February 10, 2024, https://www.beanstack.co https://www.beanstack.com/about-us/our-storym/about-us/our-story.
9. Ibid.
10. Kara Yorio, "Summer Reading Incentives: Love Them or Hate Them, Prizes Bring Kids In," *School Library Journal*, accessed February 10, 2024, https://www.slj.com/story/Summer-Reading-Incentives-Love-Them-or-Hate-Them-Prizes-Bring-Kids-In.
11. Collaborative Summer Library Program, *Why CSLP?*
12. Liz Bowie, *33 Winning Summer Reading Program Ideas*, accessed February 10, 2024, https://ideas.demco.com/blog/33-winning-summer-reading-program-ideas/.

5

Services and Resources for Children

Although each library is unique, there are core services and resources that nearly all children's library departments will feature. This chapter reviews those core elements, or the "veggies and side stuffing"—the "meat and potatoes" being storytime and summer reading programs. Areas covered include readers' advisory and reference services and building, maintaining, and displaying the collection. Also in this chapter, I'll be discussing some basic librarian "know-how" that outlines the difference between providing merely good library service to young patrons and transforming the youth department into one that offers truly exceptional service.

READERS' ADVISORY

Whether your young patron is reading their first or hundredth book, some common questions arise for which librarians need to be prepared: *What should I read now?* or *I need a good book to read; any suggestions?* or *Do you have any good books?* There are steps to answering these questions; first up is ensuring that you've read every book in your children's collection to effectively perform readers' advisory service in the library. Was that a gasp I heard? Now that I have your attention, you know it's close to impossible to read every book in the collection! Still, it's important to develop the skills needed to effectively provide advisory skills and methods for readers of all ages and experience—through both reading widely yourself and knowing your library's collection.

I've often been asked by students in the San José University iSchool about the difference between readers' advisory and the reference interview, so defining the terms will be the first consideration. Next, I'll include a bit of historical information about this service; moving on, I'll offer concrete steps to offering effective readers' advisory. While there is an art to offering readers' advisory, the task is carried out in a myriad of ways, and I will provide several options, but essentially, any way you connect readers with books is a kind of readers' advisory. Various methods of "reading" a book in a short time to know the collection better and perform the service will also be outlined, and by the end of this section, you'll have a strong foundation to help young patrons find just the right book.

READERS' ADVISORY DEFINED

Of all the definitions for readers' advisory I've come across over the years, Wikipedia provides a nice one: "Readers' advisory (sometimes spelled readers' advisory or reader's advisory) is a service which involves suggesting fiction and nonfiction titles to a reader through direct or indirect means. This service is a fundamental library service; however, readers' advisory also occurs in commercial contexts such as bookstores."[1] Thinking about doing the work of readers' advisory, I can't help but note that to provide this service, you need to know your collection. As mentioned, a librarian doesn't need to read every book to know the collection, but for me, an understanding of genres and reading areas of interest to children is important, so familiarizing yourself with your children's collection is essential. It might also be helpful to think of readers' advisory as a form of booktalking—revealing just the right amount of plot, character, and unusual elements to create an exciting reading opportunity.

The topics of books in Dewey areas in nonfiction are straightforward, but picture books and juvenile titles may be a bit trickier. First, consider how fiction is organized in your department. Are picture books arranged alphabetically by an author's last name? Maybe the picture book collection has been "genrefied," meaning they've been arranged according to genres or general concepts that may include animals, dinosaurs, transportation, nature, or school, as examples. If your library is utilizing this bookstore or retail method of arranging fiction titles according to the topic, you have a distinct advantage of getting to know the collection much better. Browse the shelves, familiarize yourself with titles, and read a few books in each of the categories; this can be done rather quickly when reading picture books, and some advice on "reading" longer titles is coming up later in this section.

About graphic novels: Please note, graphic novels are NOT a genre; they're a format, so be sure to arrange them according to the genre into which they fall. This is a pet peeve of mine, and it's important to make this distinction. If, however, you plan to group all your graphic novels in one spot, please be sure to label them with individual genres rather than grouping them as if they were a genre.

Finally, what is the difference between readers' advisory and a reference interview? In my experience, though these two services have some overlap and are often mistakenly intertwined, I experience readers' advisory as assisting patrons with their pleasure-reading needs; the reference interview focuses primarily on helping patrons find specific information about a topic. Again, this is general, but it's a good way to distinguish the two library services.

A BRIEF LOOK AT READERS' ADVISORY'S PAST

Looking back at when readers' advisory developed and charting its course over the years, you'll see that the service has had a rollercoaster of a ride in public libraries. Cited in Joyce Saricks and Nancy Brown's *Readers' Advisory Services in the Public Library*, reader's advisory service falls into three phases from the 1920s to the 1940s, as reported by Robert Ellis Lee. In its first phase, from 1922 to 1926, the readers' advisory practice, then called "reader guidance," involved a personal interview between the patron and the librarian; seven public libraries offered this service at the time. This rather official meeting was typically held in a special room, and it most closely aligns with today's reference interview.[2]

From 1927 to 1935, the second phase, readers' advisory services were in great demand and more libraries offered this service, in part because the American Library Association's (ALA) Adult Education Roundtable was founded in 1927. It's fascinating to note that despite the similarities to today's library service, librarians' focus was to educate the patron and move them into loftier academic realms; in fact, it was designed to lead them to read the classics. In addition, librarians based their recommendations to patrons, and judged their intellectual abilities and reading skills, on what magazines or newspapers the patron read.[3] Naturally, this judgment processing is not something a librarian is expected to do today, nor is it desired!

Finally, in the third phase, from 1936 to 1940, librarians were required to read widely and become subject-area specialists to serve patron's developing readers' advisory needs; librarians curated lists of books for the betterment of the patron. Here again, there was a decided attempt to label readers; seventy reader types were established, and lists were created that were used to recommend titles. Check out this verbiage: "Ranging from the Timid and Inferior-Feeling Person, The Low-Brow, and Tenement Dwellers to the Ambitious Person and Sophisticated Woman, each type was listed with three to four book titles considered appropriate reading suggestions."[4] Remarkable. It's important to note that a primary function of this service was the creation of connections between the librarian and the patron. Despite this positive result, readers' advisory outgrew the librarian's ability to keep up with demand, according to Saricks and Brown. To wrap up these three phases, with World War II and its many challenges, readers' advisory service was no longer needed and was largely suspended until forty years later. The 1980s saw readers' advisory services experience a kind of renewal attributed primarily to the ALA's Adult Reading Roundtable.[5] That brings us to present-day methods: read on!

TIPS AND TRICKS ON THE PATH TO EXPERTISE

To excel in readers' advisory, consider these time-tested tips I've accumulated over the years. Note that for some, a readers' advisory offering is instinctive, and that's great. Others might need a bit more coaching, and that's also fine. These six tips may serve as either reminders or new concepts to consider; note that the list is predominantly my own process, but when other concepts are included, they are called out with endnotes, including the work of Jessica Moyes and Katie Stover.

1. *Know your collection.* Converse with colleagues about what they read in their areas of interest that you don't share, and ask patrons what they've enjoyed in various genres; in short, talk about children's books—a LOT! Following up with that, read library journals widely and often; it'll help you become familiar with what's being published and in which genres. Read a lot yourself and stretch your comfort zones; challenge yourself to read in areas you're not typically attracted to. As an example, find outstanding science fiction if that's not normally your thing and read a truly good book in the genre. A tool that has become essential in my readers' advisory workings is recording every title I read in my LibraryThing.com account; many folks choose Goodreads, but whatever platform you use, be sure to tag titles with genres. You'll quickly realize you are your own amazing resource!

    Consider employing this quick and fun way to "read" a book. I've developed my own process here based on Jessica Moyers and Kaite Stover's checklist[6]; what follows is a blending of what I've developed over my library years merged with my instinctual approach, as I mentioned; where Moyers and Stover's information comes in, endnotes will be present.
    a. Take a moment to consider the cover—what kind of artwork am I seeing, and to what age group is this likely to be directed? Does the title help me understand the contents?
    b. Read the back-cover blurb as well as the front-flap content to get a feel for what the author and publisher intend for the book.
    c. Read the table of contents, if applicable, but certainly read the first several pages and consider the hook sentence. Does it entice the reader?
    d. Examine the book for more information: How thick is the book? How many pages?
    e. Randomly skim the text and consider the visuals: Is there artwork within the book? How friendly is the font? What is the point of view? Are there any other considerations you can ascertain as you skim?
    f. Read a couple of sections from the middle, and don't tempt your willpower, as Moyer recommends only reading the final chapter if you plan NOT to read the book.[7]

g. Finally, Moyer recommends making connections between the book in hand and other titles, and Moyer's final bit of advice is to keep a notebook populated with these ten-minute reads.[8] A notebook is great, though you might want to use your Goodreads or LibraryThing account—or perhaps create a document in Google Drive. Whatever you choose, the key is to organize the information you gather for ease of future access.

Schedule employing the above method at least once daily and you'll have created the groundwork to knowing your collection in a short time.

2. *Be approachable*! As with the reference interview, being welcoming and open to the patron and their requests sets a stage for success. A kind greeting, a smile, and a question or two about what reading preferences they have, what they read last, what they recently enjoyed, and what they may be looking for will go a long way. It's especially important that you speak to young people as equals who deserve your attention and time. In short, just use your best people skills!
3. *No cringing*. Following up being approachable, there should be no cringing. Even if it's an area you don't love, remaining neutral and invested in the patron's request is important. When someone asks for hardcore horror, trust me, I WANT to cringe, but I refrain. Also, despite not reading in this area very widely, I actively engage with fans of this genre so that I might be able to recommend a title when asked. The key is to provide your patrons with a judgment-free zone.
4. *Talk to colleagues*. Even with the method of "reading" in part one of this list, you simply cannot know everything about your collection. This is the third time I'm mentioning this because it's just that important: I often defer to a colleague who reads in a similar area even when I'm chatting with patrons. For example, I've read extensively in young adult fantasy, but I don't really read adult fantasy. A co-worker on staff is a heavy adult fantasy reader. It's fine to ask a colleague for help when working with patrons!
5. *The focus should be on the patron*. Cynthia Orr, in *Crash Course in Readers' Advisory*, reminds us that, in this process, it's not about *you*. One of your favorite books may be just what the child in front of you is looking for, or maybe not. Consider Orr's statement about this: "We have to put ourselves into our readers' shoes and try to understand what *they* like, what *they* are in the mood for, what would appeal to *them*, and not necessarily what we ourselves enjoy, or even worse, what we think they *should* read."[9] Here's another instance when listening skills come in handy, and when it comes to assisting patrons, *listening is key*.

6. *Utilize other resources.* Librarians have a vast selection of assets to help with readers' advisory; aside from familiarizing yourself with your own collection, two standout resources are my "go-to" for help when I'm stuck.
    a. Novelist Plus, an electronic service provided by many libraries through subscription, is truly exceptional. Once logged into your library's account, there are options to select the age level you'd like—adult, teen, ages nine to twelve, and ages newborn to eight—and further divisions permit the user to select "All Kinds of Lives," as one example, which includes further distinctions such as LGBTQ+ Kids' Lives, Muslim Kids' Lives, and Disabled Kids' Lives, among others. Novelist Plus also offers the ability to key in a book title that the patron loved, such as *Charlotte's Web*, and in the results list, *Charlotte's Web* is the first listing, and clicking on "Title Read-alikes" yields a list of titles, which, in this case, includes *Pax* by Sara Pennypacker and *The Wild Robot* by Peter Brown. One may also click on "Author Read-alikes" to discover authors who write in a similar tone and focus; for this example, two results include Beverly Cleary and Randall Jarrell.[10] If your library has this powerful resource, become familiar with it!
    b. Next, consider the free and easily accessed whatshouldireadnext.com. Here again, performing the search for *Charlotte's Web* results includes over forty titles along with cover images. A few of these results include *Ramona Forever* by Beverly Cleary, *The Tale of Peter Rabbit* by Beatrix Potter, *Mrs. Frisby and the Rats of NIMH* by Robert O'Brien, *Pippi Longstocking* by Astrid Lindgren, and *Charlie and the Great Glass Elevator* by Roald Dahl.[11] If you're familiar with these classic titles, you may agree as I did with the common themes, and therefore, they are excellent recommendations. From time to time, I search random book titles on this site just to better familiarize myself with read-alikes to learn just what is in my own collection. It's all about familiarity with the collection!

READERS' ADVISORY AND CAREGIVERS

One final section on readers' advisory that must be noted involves the presence of caregivers during a readers' advisory session. It's wonderful that caregivers are invested in their children's reading, but in some cases, it can be tricky. Well-meaning caregivers may seek to help their children select books, so navigating this dynamic is a delicate process; my rule of thumb is to direct questions and conversation directly to the child. I avoid speaking with the caregiver as though the child is not present. By engaging in conversation with the child, particularly when they're reading in the juvenile section, and acknowledging the caregiver, all parties will be respected. Caregivers of very young children often make selections for their children, so it's important to not only build up readers' advisory skills with young patrons, but one must also interact well with adults.

REFERENCE SERVICES

Now that I've explored concepts of reader's advisory, next up is an exploration of reference services. I'll begin with a little story.

I'm not proud of this, but as a brand-new and very green librarian, I found the study of the reference process to be kind of silly. Isn't it just a quick conversation about finding a dinosaur book or a title on the planets for a school assignment? Why are entire books written on the topic? Then I took a reference services course and wised up. Now better informed, I'll be touching on the history, the definition, and key elements of reference services rather than diving into details, but reference services are constantly in flux, and the librarian is on an unending path to refine this library offering. Consider the development of technology, specifically the Internet and Google. While this may have shifted users' needs for a librarian a bit, as patrons can conduct their own searches, it's quite clear that a well-trained reference librarian can offer resources that a user may overlook. The librarian continues to be an important part of the reference service; training in evaluating resources for accuracy has never been more important.

A BRIEF HISTORY OF YOUTH REFERENCE SERVICES

A history of children's services in the public library was outlined earlier in this book, but it is not surprising that the gradual recognition of children and their information needs align with the development of reference services. The dawn of the 1800s saw a need to offer specialized services to youth. Over time, librarians worked closely with teachers to provide support for classroom assignments—this relationship with schools became more prevalent in the 1900s and, according to Rees in Kay Cassell's *Reference and Information Services: An Introduction*, involved "the sharing of book collections, presentations by public librarians to schoolchildren on public library resources, organized school visits to the public library, and assignment alerts given to the public library by teachers."[12] Cassell notes that after the 1957 launch of the Soviet Union's Sputnik 1, the first artificial Earth satellite, the United States was in a bit of a tailspin thinking they were falling behind with children's education; Russia had been the first to launch! With that, government funding for schools increased, and eventually, the Internet made a big impact on reference services. Not surprisingly, as was the case in the 1900s, public library reference service now directly supports school efforts and works to assist with academic efforts.[13]

REFERENCE SERVICES: A DEFINITION AND GENERAL OVERVIEW

Wikipedia will once again set the stage with this definition: "A reference interview is a conversation between a librarian and a library user, usually at a reference desk, in which the librarian responds to the user's initial explanation of his or her information need by first attempting to clarify that need and then by directing the user to appropriate information resources."[14] That's a great foundation, but attached to that are ethical considerations required to do the work well. Kay Ann Cassell and Uma Hiremath outline a librarian's knowledge and understanding of the ALA's Code of Ethics as the underpinning for good reference work—the librarian must strive to provide accurate information without bias, and to be courteous—providing all users with equal attention and care. Note the deeper dive into the Code of Ethics mentioned by Cassell and Hiremath: "The code calls for upholding the principles of intellectual freedom and resisting attempts to censor library materials."[15] Harkening back to that readers' advisory interaction, using people skills and being welcoming, open, and nonjudgmental are all requirements for this type of interaction as well.

In addition to adhering to a code of ethics, the librarian needs to constantly update their knowledge of resources available—what works, what doesn't, what's reliable, what isn't. This is an ongoing process of self-education, and in addition, specifically for youth, the librarian must understand the basic workings of children at various age levels. In fact, an intricate web of skills is needed for this library service. While a young person may be independently pursuing a topic of interest, it's more often that reference questions pertain to schoolwork. More on homework help later; the key here is that the public librarian can be much more effective through creating connections with the school librarian and classroom teachers.

In the reference interview, the librarian not only answers the patron's question but, often, is required to tease out the details of what the patron is looking for; they are not always sure of their actual information needs, so a good bit of sleuthing is required on the part of the librarian.

OFFERING EXCEPTIONAL REFERENCE SERVICES: THE BASICS

Reflecting on my time in the youth department, I concur with Cassell's assertion that nearly all questions from youth are directional[16]—they want to know where to find books on a particular topic or where they could find specific information. Reference services are a bit more than this. Typically, a young person, much like their adult counterparts, isn't entirely certain of exactly what their information needs are; therefore, the librarian must don a detective hat. First, the librarian's task is to listen carefully, then begin carefully constructing questions to help the patron work out their needs. If the librarian has an established role with the school, some assignment information may have already been shared. If not, the detective work may be challenging, but with practice, the reference interview can be mastered and is ultimately rewarding.

A good start to reiterating the elements of the reference interview is enumerated in the National Archives at Boston's guidelines. In fact, there are five easy steps to consider, which I've outlined here; I recommend you seek out the document and deepen your understanding in your quest to develop a strong skill base.

First, as with any library transaction, be approachable! A welcoming demeanor that does not pass judgment will put patrons at ease; this includes making eye contact, issuing a greeting, and moving toward the patron to indicate your willingness to help. Carefully listening to the questions asked will help guide the discussion and ultimate discovery of needs, but be sure to engage with the person in front of you before hitting the computer. After offering help on a topic, your patron is likely to do some initial exploring. Always check back to see if the information you helped them find was effective and then repeat the "listen and question" steps if your young patron needs more assistance.

The remaining guidelines are the following: (2) show an interest in the patron's questions—this just makes good sense; (3) exercise good listening skills, and to let the patron know you've heard the request, repeat that information back, but only after you've listened carefully and fully to the patron's request; (4) searching is the next step, and this is when the librarian pairs knowledge with what has just been ascertained from the patron questions. A good search, obviously, will yield helpful results. Here, demonstrate searching skills and offer additional suggestions to have them explore on their own (depending on the age of the patron); (5) finally, in the last step, check in with the patron once again to ensure informational needs have been met.[17] Finesse is needed, and good communication skills are paramount. Connect with the people in front of you, and you're more likely to be successful.

HOMEWORK HELP

As mentioned in the discussion of the reference interview, schoolwork can easily lead to interactions with your student patrons. Aside from assisting with topical guidance, the youth department can be a haven for young patrons to work on their homework in a quiet and supportive setting.

Homework help for the youth department varies from the simple provision of materials and space for a young patron to do their homework—pencils, markers, paper, rulers, and so on—to a formal level of service. Thinking back to my own years in elementary and middle school, I relished homework and loved the challenge of working things out on my own. This isn't the case for all students. For those who need additional assistance, having to do homework could cause anxiety and frustration. The library can help.

As a youth librarian, I often had students check in with me about what a particular question on their homework meant or whether an answer was right or not. I was happy to engage in this conversation, and the homework assistance offered was an informal chat. The library's Friends group funded the stocking of a homework cart with all manner of school supplies; however, the community need for deeper homework assistance was not present, and this homework help approach worked by meeting the needs of my community.

When either creating a homework help center or assessing whether what's being offered in the library is adequate, take a hard look at the community as a first step. As in so many other areas of library service, knowing the community dynamic and assessing the needs of youth in your area is of utmost importance; you may consider a survey of some kind, chatting with caregivers, and connecting with the school to assess needs. Your discovery may lead you to find that, like my own library, providing supplies is sufficient, but after an informal survey of larger libraries around the country, there are vast and involved programs that offer a wide range of homework assistance, from one-on-one assistance via paid or volunteer adults to a vast array of online resources. A search at the New York Public Library yielded twenty-one results in the homework-help area; of note is their offering of Brainfuze, real-time help with a live tutor available from 2:00 p.m. to 11:00 p.m. Eastern, whose statement reads: "Interact with live tutors in math, science, reading/writing, social studies, PSAT/SAT, ACT, AP and state standardized tests."[18]

What level of homework assistance is needed in your area? If you're already offering homework help, is it time to evaluate its effectiveness and make changes to suit your community's needs?

COLLECTION DEVELOPMENT AND DEACCESSION

Collection development and deaccession, or weeding, is a vast and wondrous area of librarianship. In both developing and weeding the collection, you are making decisions for the community, which, in this case, are young patrons from birth through eighth grade. Although the development and weeding of the collection may be a fundamental concept, it may prove to be more challenging than you imagine.

Collection development, for me, is a gift. I was one of those kids who loved it when the Scholastic book orders arrived—that box of books on the teacher's desk always held so much appeal to me. Today, it's not much different. I love discovering new titles and adding them to the collection, and getting a box of new books is like a joyous holiday. Weeding was initially a fun process—until I had to start removing titles that I had purchased. This was painful, at least at first. Now, I take the perspective that weeding a book I thought would work for the community but didn't is nothing more than a learning opportunity. I have librarian friends who love the process of weeding, and there are those who loathe it. After all these years, it feels great to weed—get rid of what's not working to bring in what will.

KNOWING YOUR COMMUNITY

One of the keys to collection development is knowing your community. Are you recognizing a theme with this first bit of advice? All services and community offerings are driven by community needs; I can't state it enough! Certainly, time spent with patrons helps, but if you're new to your community and to the library, one of the first guiding documents to consider is the library's strategic plan. In developing a strategic plan, the library may have conducted a patron survey to get input on various library services, input on the collection, and feedback on community needs. This information would help inform a needs assessment, which, in turn, would guide staff to make decisions about service, programs, and, naturally, the collection. By speaking with library colleagues who may have participated in this work, you can gain some insights into developing the collection.

SELF-CENSORSHIP IN COLLECTION DEVELOPMENT AND DEACCESSION

Self-censorship occurs when a librarian makes judgment-based decisions about the collection based not on community needs but for other reasons. Those decisions may be based on fear, perceived values, the concept that the librarian knows best, or other pressures. We all have inherent biases; it's part of human nature. Regardless, those biases must be set aside when curating and maintaining a library collection for youth. Sounds easy, but as I learned early on, the challenge is real!

Allow my personal story to illustrate this point. Years ago, as a new librarian, I purchased a title for the young adult collection, and if I'm honest, the catalyst for purchase was the cover as well as the popularity of the author at the time. The book arrived, and I noticed details on the cover I had originally missed, and they indicated a more sinister tale than I had anticipated. In fact, Elizabeth Scott's book *Living Dead Girl* was one I brought home and stood at my dining room table reading—I didn't even sit down. I devoured it in the same way a person can't look away from a fiery car accident. I struggled after reading this horrific tale of the abduction and abuse of a young girl from her grade-school field trip. It was so difficult for me to read, and I immediately decided that I couldn't put it on the shelf. I was so distraught that I contacted the author and asked the reasoning behind publishing a book like this. While the answer she provided was sound, I still couldn't get past the content to put it on the shelf. Finally, I called our New Hampshire State Library children's librarian, and we chatted. She helped me see that not all books are for all readers, that the book did, in fact, belong in the collection, and that I should shelve it. All this to illustrate that what I thought may not be a good title to add to the library collection due to my own horror over a young person reading the book, I quickly learned that this was not *my* collection. This book had a purpose, and someone in the community may benefit from its place on the shelf. I keep reminding my graduate school students when I discuss collection development that the sign over the library door reads RYE PVBLIC LIBRARY [this is the actual spelling], not "Lisa's Library." This experience led me to reflect on two collection development issues: first, self-censorship in collection development, and second, what would guide me as a youth librarian in collection development.

During this writing, the number of challenges being brought forth in the United States is astronomical—never seen in the history of the country. PBS reports that "More than 1,200 challenges were compiled by the association in 2022, nearly double the then-record total from 2021 and by far the most since the ALA began keeping data 20 years ago."[19] The climate of anger and challenges to books can create fear in librarians who may opt to remove books from the shelf in advance of a potential issue or may even refrain from purchasing titles. This is self-censorship, also called soft censorship. Kelly Jensen breaks down the definition: "Quiet censorship—also known as soft censorship or self-censorship, terms used interchangeably—is when materials are purposefully removed, limited, or never purchased at all despite it being a title that would serve a community. This is not a new issue, but now, with more 'parental rights' groups demanding curricular and collection oversight, even the best professionals who don't believe in censorship are falling victim to choosing the path of considering the people who may complain over those who may need the material."[20] This is a fitting reminder as we take a closer look at collection development.

Check yourself for your own biases often, and remember that decisions you make directly impact the people of your community who need representation on the library's shelves; your task is to uphold the tenets of intellectual freedom and provide equitable access to information. If fear of community backlash is influencing your collection development, then consider basing collection decisions on a collection development policy. This will help you remove your own personal beliefs from decision-making and insulate you from individual complaints about materials. More on this will be discussed in the chapter on intellectual freedom.

COLLECTION DEVELOPMENT POLICY

Does your library have a policy? If it does, take some time to read it carefully. Compare the policy to resources in the *Intellectual Freedom Manual* of the ALA to ensure your library's policy covers all needed elements. A solid, well-crafted policy, here based on my library's policy, is one that includes the following sections: philosophy; objectives of selection; responsibility for selection; criteria for selection; selection (resources used for materials selection); collection maintenance; policy on controversial materials; challenged materials; a reconsideration form; perhaps a placement policy outlining that although materials are separated by age group, everyone may use materials in all areas of the library; and finally, an outline of weeding practices that include how to weed items gifted to the library.

To summarize, the policy specifies that the library serves all people, includes guidelines around how materials are purchased, with what criteria, how they are maintained, and how they are weeded—and all this should tie to the library's mission statement. Another key element of the policy is the inclusion of the Freedom to Read Statement—that all people are free to read without censorship, and the collection will necessarily include diverse materials that may be objectionable to some readers. One very critical element, especially for the youth department, is to include a statement specifying that the library does not function *in loco parentis*; in other words, the library is not acting in the place of a parent or guardian by limiting their reading.

If you find your library's policy is lacking or you are starting from scratch, survey various policies from several libraries in your area or state, especially those you admire. They should be available on their websites. Formulate a policy that ensures both staff and patrons' rights are protected and include a section on staff training on the concepts of intellectual freedom. Whether you discover your library already has a thorough and useful selection development policy or work with staff on developing one, use well-established policies as tools to help you avoid potential self-censorship and protect the library from banning attempts.

BUILDING AND MAINTAINING THE COLLECTION

When considering who selects titles for the collection, I've found that it takes a village. Employ the expertise of your staff to assist in developing a collection that serves the community. Route copies of resources like the *School Library Journal* or *The Horn Book* to all staff to get their contributions. Your collection will be richer and far more diverse than if only one person chooses materials.

I've mentioned two resources for collection development, but these may be somewhat limiting. To ensure a richly diverse collection, consider searching in other sources, for example, "We Need Diverse Books," Cooperative Children's Book Center, Lee & Low Books, and the ALA's Children's Book Council. Read blogs like "I'm Here, I'm Queer, What the Hell Do I Read?" and "American Indians in Children's Literature." I've found a specific search for diverse titles in any given area will yield a myriad of results, and I have found excellent titles when searching independent publishers. Get creative, and don't limit yourself to the "big five" publishers.

Conducting an audit of your collection, especially with a look at diversity, is an ongoing and important task. Michael Sullivan, in *Children's Services, Second Edition*, nicely encapsulates the full range of collection tasks from purchase to eventual weeding: "Managing a modern collection means choosing what belongs, not just on the day it was purchased but every day after that."[21] When you're interested in an in-depth analysis of your collection, consider reading through *The Complete Collections Assessment Manual: A Holistic Approach* by Madeline Kelly.[22] Another good foundational text devoted to youth collection development that includes thirteen tools or forms among other beneficial information is *Collection Management for Youth: Equity, Inclusion, and Learning* by Sandra Hughes-Hassel.[23]

Also, under the umbrella of building the collection, consider the budget to help prioritize acquisitions of all materials, including books, audiobooks, digital resources, DVDs, and more. To work out a budget, consider the cost of materials—prices of books increase continuously; the size of the collection, what items are in demand, and if the library needs to purchase more than one copy of popular books; consider replacement and repair costs; and ensure that your collection is accessible to all—large-print materials and audiobooks, for example, provide access to a wider population.

SHELVING THE COLLECTION—ARE YOU READY FOR DYNAMIC SHELVING?

As a starting point, I will assert that the library's primary purpose is to inspire interest in materials and to provide accessibility to those same materials. With that in mind, I invite you to take a hard look at how your materials are arranged, and considering your young readers, ask how "findable" those materials are. Simple question, right? In researching display and shelving options, I have found there are very exciting possibilities for youth collections. I must warn you now that it may require a massive shift in thinking and buy-in from library colleagues, but before you make a judgment, join me in considering some new possibilities.

Recently, picture books in my library's collection were moved from the typical alphabetical last name shelving format to a genre format. Think about children's information needs; what would be easier to find when searching for, say, trucks? The alphabetical format would require the child to search the catalog, find the book, then locate the author's last name. Now consider the same kid who loves trucks coming into the library and knowing that the books she loves reading have a green spine label and are collected in one area called "Go." Which is more accessible?

I attended an engaging presentation on how to shelve a library collection presented at the New Hampshire Library Association conference in May of 2023, and I have to say, I was excited, even ecstatic! As I walked out of that session, my mind was whirling with possibilities. Lucia Von Letkemann's *No More Static Shelves! Making Your Collection More Dynamic and Less Daunting* presentation included three areas to explore in exciting, user-friendly, non-traditional shelving: Genrefication, the Bookstore/Retail Model, and the Dynamic Shelving Model.[24] Before getting to that and beginning the process of changing shelving practices, Von Letkemann advises beginning with weeding and taking inventory. Though some despise the practice, Von Letkemann expounds on the "life-changing magic" of weeding! Talk about an enthusiastic perspective! Weeding will be examined more closely later in this chapter. For now, just know that doing this prior to making shelving changes will be of great benefit.[25]

GENREFYING YOUR SHELVES

Simply stated, as I understand it, "genrefying" is a classification system in which books are shelved according to their genre rather than by author or title. The concept is used in bookstores in a way as titles are grouped in nonfiction, and this method enables the shopper to browse in an area of interest more easily and encourages sales. When used in the public library, the library patron benefits for similar reasons—the shelves are more browsable, and rather than increased sales, expect increased circulation. Materials are more easily found, and browsing capabilities are increased. Overhauling the entire collection to fit this model will likely be a huge undertaking, but the benefits far outweigh the time investment. The drawbacks I've encountered here include more time-consuming shelving for the librarian as well as an inability to quickly find a book when you're not sure of the genre. In this case, heading to the catalog to see where the book is shelved is required.

Feeling overwhelmed about adopting this approach? You should! Depending on the size of your collection, this could be a daunting undertaking, but if you break it down into bite-sized bits, it is less of a mountain to climb. Von Letkemann recommends selecting just one genre to focus on as a start. As an example, pull out mysteries, give them their own area, and see how it goes. You can give this a try as a pilot experiment and have patrons and staff weigh in. It may be effective for some communities, but it may not meet the needs of your community, and that's okay, according to Von Letkemann. Use color and clear signage by labeling both the shelves and the book spines for even more visibility. Drawbacks to this method include resistance from staff, the extreme amount of time and energy needed to make this change, and the actual process of determining into which genre each title must go.[26]

BOOKSTORE/RETAIL MODEL

You've likely seen this method of shelving when visiting your local bookstore. To sell titles, they need to be seen, so you'll frequently see books face out—the cover is on full display. Even if we think we're immune, this old adage is pretty much true for everyone, though we all seem to do it: "You can't judge a book by its cover." Showing those covers increases sales, and it was mentioned that when Amazon had physical bookstores, ALL books were shelved face out. Think about your shelves at the library; are they crammed tight—so packed it's hard to remove a title without three others falling out with it? If that's the case, you'll need to weed, and as I've promised, more on that later in this chapter. It's probably not possible to adopt Amazon's face-out model in the library, but clearing out shelves, having breathing room, and including as many titles face out as possible will increase circulation. Consider using slatwalls at the end of shelving units for even more visibility—just as you might see at your local bookstore. Of the three shelving methods mentioned, this is by far the most attainable; you just need to weed, shift, and create visibility.

Drawbacks to using this method include utilizing more space than the non-traditional method, and maintaining and shelving books can be more challenging for the librarian. Still, the benefit to patrons just may outweigh these drawbacks.[27]

DYNAMIC SHELVING

This is perhaps the most exciting of all options as it encompasses the concepts of genrefying and the retail model but adds additional elements to create excitement around books. Although for this section I'm highlighting Kelsey Bogan's work, a high school librarian and fellow instructor at San José State University, these ideas are specific to shelving books for teens and can be applied to other age groups.

Heading to Bogan's blog "Don't Shush Me: Adventures of a 21st Century High School Librarian," you'll find detailed information on dynamic shelving, among many other topics; I've been working in libraries since 2006, and I have to say, Bogan's work has deeply inspired me—you won't want to miss her blog.[28]

Bogan differentiates between "static shelving" and "dynamic shelving." Static shelving, what most libraries have "always used," is described as boring, uninspiring, and potentially confusing; its purpose is to make the librarian's job easier. Dynamic shelving, on the other hand, creates excitement, interest, and increases the chance young patrons will walk out of the library with one or more books. Bogan's site includes images illustrating the difference between the shelving types; dynamic shelving includes the option of painting the shelves of each genre a specific color, creating open space on the shelves, piling series books behind the first in the series, and ensuring each shelf features multiple face-out titles. For those piled books, Bogan has even created a unique way to ensure that the first front-faced title stays in place: use a bookend placed inside the book to hold it in place.[29]

Looking at a Demco presentation created by Bogan, dynamic shelving is defined as "A philosophy of embracing flexibility and a marketing-mindset in our library organization strategies so we may provide collections that are more *accessible* and *independently navigable* to the average library user . . . To help us demystify the library and remove barriers of access common within traditional (archaic) library organization systems."[30] This is exciting!

Aesthetically, dynamic shelving is just gorgeous; it makes my librarian heart sing! Pops of color, clear and colorful signage, décor (consider sitting a Mo Willems stuffed pigeon on the shelf near the pigeon books), and including "shelf talkers"—these ideas go a long way to enticing readers. If this isn't enough, and if you're maybe thinking that the way you've always done it is fine, the statistics Bogan supplies cannot be disputed; Bogan recorded circulation statistics every September between 2017 and 2022, and aside from a dip in circulation numbers during the pandemic, there was a 900 percent increase in circulation during the first month of school before and after the high school adopted dynamic shelving. That's right! Not 9 percent or 90 percent—a full 900 percent increase![31]

As with the earlier advice on adopting a new shelving plan, Bogan notes that starting small is the best way to begin by implementing various techniques to see what works and what doesn't. Avoid purchasing materials for this project and use what's readily available in your library, and finally, Bogan encourages librarians to focus on what *can* be done.[32] As many libraries are limited by their budget, starting out small and using materials on hand is a great way to test the waters with patrons and skeptical colleagues. As part of the test, you may want to create performance measures, such as examining browsing times as well as comparing circulation statistics before and after the changes were made. This data is a great way to report to staff the value of a new shelving system.

Von Letkemann notes that there are drawbacks to this shelving option as well. Here, they include a distinct adjustment period for staff as the shelves may not be as "clean" as librarians are used to seeing; also, more shelf space is needed for this method, perhaps even more if décor is included; the requirement for creativity and flexibility from staff; and the need for more shelf maintenance.[33] If your budget is restrictive and time is your only resources, find ways to make changes to benefit your patrons; they'll likely thank you for it!

Before undertaking a major project, I'd like to add that if you're in a position of authority, seek the opinions of your staff, engage them in the process, and be forthcoming about your enthusiasm. Talk with them about the benefits and shortcomings of making a big change like this and seek out their feedback and ideas. This avoids potential resentment and frustration. Further, it helps connect you to your staff and supports an environment of collaboration. This way, the entire team will be involved!

WEEDING, AKA DEACCESSION

I have librarian friends who LIVE for weeding. They'd almost rather do this than any other library work! Not everyone shares this passion. Rebecca Vnuk has a line that has stuck with me since reading *The Weeding Handbook: A Shelf-by-Shelf Guide*. It goes like this: "The very word weeding often strikes terror in a librarian's heart."[34] As I've mentioned, I also enjoyed weeding as a new librarian until I had to weed books *I had purchased*—that was a bit more difficult. Since then, and after learning about CREW and MUSTIE methods and reading Vnuk's literal shelf-by-shelf guide, I've come to appreciate the task for several reasons, and it's an important task.

First, and most obviously, is space management. If a library continues to expand the collection without a physical building expansion, it will eventually overflow with books that are likely not even circulating. I entitle the week in my course focused on weeding "It's All About the Real Estate" for a reason! Shelf space is limited, and making room for new materials is paramount. Perhaps think of it this way: out with the "old friends," and in with the "new friends." To soften the blow of weeding, remember that when you donate books or even have a library book sale, those "old friends" will find a happy new home.

Second, if the shelves are stuffed with books, it's likely some of them are outdated and no longer relevant—some may even contain inaccurate information; consider books on geography—borders change more often than you realize, and think about the downgraded status of Pluto—how many titles are still on the shelf with the erroneous information that Pluto is a planet? Additionally, those stuffed shelves do not encourage circulation; the titles simply aren't adequately accessible. Think back to the section on Dynamic Shelving where circulation is increased; packed shelves circulate poorly and require librarians to shelf-shift when re-shelving. Opening those shelves saves time! Also, during the weeding process, the librarian notes titles that need to be repaired or replaced, and I weed and take inventory simultaneously—as I think most librarians do.

Third, weeding helps the librarian to identify gaps in the collection, and so the process itself informs areas that need attention. I recently weeded and realized that though we had many books on World War II, many no longer circulated, were outdated, and more recent titles were needed to "beef up" that nonfiction area.

Fourth and finally, weeding helps the librarian identify titles that have a short life on the shelf; in other words, frequent weeding informs future purchases by indicating certain areas that may become obsolete too quickly or are just not the right fit for their communities.

The very best resource for weeding is the Texas State Library and Archives Commission's manual *CREW: A Weeding Manual for Modern Libraries*. In fact, their entire website includes extensive resources on weeding. The CREW acronym helps outline further details in the weeding process: Continuous Review, Evaluation, and Weeding. The manual is available online at https://www.tsl.texas.gov/ld/pubs/crew/index.html. In my own library, I've printed it in its entirety (108 pages), placed it in its own binder, and have required staff who do weeding to read it.

The last mention here is the MUSTIE method, a guiding process in weeding.

"MUSTIE is the acronym for six negative factors that make books prime candidates for weeding."[35]

- M—Misleading (and/or factually inaccurate): Weed outdated editions and books that are no longer accurate. Pay special attention to areas where information has changed recently or where it changes rapidly, like in medicine and travel.
- U—Ugly: This is probably self-evident, but a book that looks bad, is worn out, and beyond mending needs to be removed from the shelf.
- S—Superseded (by a truly new edition or by a much better book on the subject): Especially for reference materials, test guides, and travel manuals, weed older editions. Most public libraries don't need to keep older editions for research value.
- T—Trivial (of no discernible literary or scientific merit; usually of ephemeral interest at some time in the past): Weed older titles that are of fleeting interest or are about outdated popular culture.
- I—Irrelevant to the needs and interests of your community.
- E—Elsewhere: The material or information may be obtained expeditiously elsewhere. Especially for items available at no cost, such as through Project Gutenberg, don't clutter the library catalog with material that is not being used or is out of date. On the other hand, you may decide to weed some physical copies of classic literature that are infrequently used if the books are available through a free eBook source like Project Gutenberg.[36]

While the CREW method is a gold standard, Vnuk's weeding handbook mentioned at the beginning of this section includes a humorous weeding "skit" and offers, as the title states, guides for weeding in all shelves of the library with a chapter dedicated to youth collections and some common pitfalls and advice for the youth librarian; I recommend reading it cover to cover if you're in the position of weeding. It's a bit less cumbersome and lengthy than the CREW manual, so it's a good starting point.

Some final thoughts on weeding include finding ways to make the job fun. One of my staff and I used to print our weeding report, one of us would stand at the stacks and check the titles, and the other sat with a clipboard and the report, making notes. While doing this, we'd have a friendly competition to see how many titles we'd read from each of the shelf areas. Occasionally, we'd come across a book that we just knew should be in the collection despite not circulating; the person who was most attached to the book would make note of it, include it in a display, and attempt to hand-sell the title. In the next weeding round, if it hadn't circulated, it was weeded. Once you've seen the impacts that a soundly weeded collection can have, you'll appreciate the effort and the breathing room.

YOUTH MEDIA AWARDS

The final section of this chapter is an examination of youth media awards. If you've ever had the privilege of heading to an ALA Annual Conference, you'll quickly see the frenzy of excitement around each year's announcement of Youth Media Award winners. I looked around at the first ceremony I attended and felt like I was at a Van Halen concert—I understand that mentioning that band dates me, so maybe compare that to a Taylor Swift concert and you get the idea: oh my goodness, the screaming! Librarians can truly be enthusiastic about books!

In my young adult materials course, students are required to examine teen awards and discuss whether teens themselves care about the awards or are in any way influenced by them in their reading. The overwhelming evidence points to them not caring very much. Librarians love the Youth Media Awards (I certainly do!), authors love the awards, and recognizing exceptional literature is valid, but not all age groups derive the same benefit. In another story, I can speak to the impact that our New Hampshire Great Stone Face Award for grades four to six has had; those kids loved getting a list of books to read in spring, would read them over the year, vote in the fall, and eagerly await the announcement of the winning title. Appreciation of the awards is relative.

While the American Library Association Youth Media Awards, which include the Caldecott, Newbery, Stonewall, and Printz awards, among others, are the major players, it's important to seek out the vast field of awards beyond ALA; consider the Walter Dean Myers award that recognizes "diverse authors whose works feature diverse main characters and address diversity in a meaningful way"[37] and the American Indian Youth Literature Award. Including titles from these resources and others will provide patrons with a diverse selection of award-winning children's literature.

The major ALA awards are not without controversy. A simple search will yield articles that raise more questions than the benefits that the awards provide. I'm personally invested in the awards and get as excited as the next librarian when they're announced, especially when I've read widely in the age category—the anticipation I feel is real.

Be sure to check out the awards in your state. I was able to serve on two award committees over the years—one for teens, and one for middle-grade titles—and the experience was incredibly, well, rewarding (pardon the pun), though I've never read so much at one time in my life!

So much of what we do as librarians is considered the heart of librarianship, but readers' advisory and reference interviews and other daily interactions with young patrons comprise most of the work; finding joy in these interactions will help you create a welcoming atmosphere that tells kids that you care about and are there to help them. This is the work!

REVIEW QUESTIONS

1. What is the distinction between readers' advisory and reference services?
2. Discuss necessary library skills for effective readers' advisory and reference services.
3. Head to the National Archives at Boston online and dig more deeply into the guidelines for effective reference interviews; report on at least two areas of interest that you discovered.
4. In nearly all library services and offerings, what is mentioned in this chapter and others about the most important consideration that the librarian must make? Discuss.
5. Define self-censorship and explore the concept further with deeper research; outline your findings.
6. Carefully read the collection development policy of your work library or the library in your hometown; compare it to the guidelines in ALA's *Intellectual Freedom Manual*. How does the existing policy measure up to ALA's checklist?
7. What are the three shelving options mentioned in this chapter? Outline the benefits and potential setbacks of each. Would you consider any of these options; why or why not?
8. Explore the CREW Weeding Manual by heading to the website. Note areas that are especially illuminating.
9. What is the controversy around youth media awards?

NOTES

1. Wikipedia, "Readers' Advisory," accessed April 30, 2023, https://en.wikipedia.org/wiki/Readers%27_advisory.
2. Joyce G. Saricks and Nancy Brown, *Readers' Advisory Service in the Public Library, 2nd Edition* (Chicago and London: American Library Association, 1997), 4.
3. Ibid., 3.
4. Ibid., 4.
5. Juris Divelko and Candice F. C. Magowan, *Readers' Advisory Service in North American Public Libraries 1975 to 2005: A History and Critical Analysis* (Jefferson, NC: McFarland & Company, Inc., Publishers, 2007), 3.
6. Jessica E. Moyer & Kaite Mediatore Stover, eds., *The Readers' Advisory Handbook* (Chicago: American Library Association, 2010), 7.
7. Ibid., 5.
8. Ibid., 6.
9. Cynthia Orr, *Crash Course in Readers' Advisory* (Santa Barbara, CA: Libraries Unlimited, 2015), 78.
10. Novelist Plus, "Charlotte's Web," accessed April 28, 2023, https://web.p.ebscohost.com/novp/results?nobk=y&vid=10&sid=f5f0ef31-19be-40a8-8ac4-a4bc933fa4b5%40redis&bquery=Charlotte%2527s%2520Web&bdata=JnR5cGU9MCZzZWFyY2hNb2RlPUFuZCZzaXRlPW5vdnAtbGl2ZQ%3d%3d.

11. What Should I Read Next? *"Charlotte's Web,"* accessed April 28, 2023, https://web.p.ebscohost.com/novp/results?nobk=y&vid=10&sid=f5f0ef31-19be-40a8-8ac4-a4bc933fa4b5%40redis&bquery=Charlotte%2527s%2520Web&bdata=JnR5cGU9MCZzZWFyY2hNb2RlPUFuZCZzaXRlPW5vdnAtbGl2ZQ%3d%3d.
12. Kay Ann Cassell and Uma Hiremath, *Reference and Information Services: An Introduction, 3rd Edition* (Chicago: Neal-Schuman, an Imprint of the American Library Association, 2013), 304.
13. Ibid., 304.
14. Wikipedia. "Reference Interview," accessed May 1, 2023, https://en.wikipedia.org/wiki/Reference_interview.
15. Cassell and Hiremath, *Reference and Information Services*, 4.
16. Ibid., 305.
17. The National Archives at Boston, "Guidelines of the Successful Reference Interview from American Library Association," accessed May 5, 2023, https://www.archives.gov/files/boston/volunteers/reference-interviews.pdf.
18. New York Public Library, "Brainfuze," accessed May 1, 2023, https://landing.brainfuse.com/authenticate.asp?u=main.nypl.ny.brainfuse.com.
19. PBS News Hour, "Book Ban Attempts Reach Record High in 2022, American Library Association Report Says," accessed May 5, 2023, https://www.pbs.org/newshour/arts/book-ban-attempts-reach-record-high-in-2022-american-library-association-report-says.
20. Kelly Jensen, "Soft and Quiet: Self-Censorship in an Era of Book Challenges," accessed May 5, 2023, https://bookriot.com/what-is-soft-or-quiet-censorship/.
21. Michael Sullivan, *Fundamentals of Children's Services*, 2nd Edition (Chicago: American Library Association, 2013), 44.
22. Madeline M. Kelly, *The Collections Assessment Manual: A Holistic Approach*. (Chicago: ALA Neal-Schuman, 2021).
23. Sandra Hughes-Hassell, *Collection Management for Youth: Equity, Inclusion, and Learning*, 2nd Edition (Chicago: ALA Editions, 2020).
24. Lucia Von Letkemann, "No More Static Shelves! Making Your Collection More Dynamic and Less Daunting," presented at the New Hampshire Library Association's Spring Conference, May 5, 2023, Meredith, New Hampshire.
25. Ibid.
26. Ibid.
27. Ibid.
28. Kelsey Bogan, "Dynamic Shelving Pt. 1: Introducing Dynamic Shelving," accessed May 10, 2023, https://dontyoushushme.com/2022/02/28/embracing-dynamic-shelving/.
29. Ibid.
30. Kelsey Bogan, "Demco Ideas & Inspiration Webinar, Dynamic Shelving with Kelsey Bogan," accessed May 10, 2023, https://www.canva.com/design/DAFcj8NMENE/ZH8y3noxMtSrAiM0FKsvPw/view?utm_content=DAFcj8NMENE&utm_campaign=designshare&utm_medium=link&utm_source=publishsharelink#6.
31. Ibid.
32. Ibid.
33. Von Letkemann, "No More Static Shelves!"

34. Rebecca Vnuk, *The Weeding Handbook: A Shelf-by-Shelf Guide* (Chicago: ALA Editions, 2022).
35. Texas State Library and Archives Commission, "CREW: A Weeding Manual for Modern Libraries," 52, 53, accessed May 10, 2023, https://www.tsl.texas.gov/sites/default/files/public/tslac/ld/ld/pubs/crew/crewmethod12.pdf.
36. Ibid., 52.
37. WNDB, "The Walter Awards," accessed May 5, 2023, https://diversebooks.org/programs/walter-awards/.

6

The Welcoming and Inclusive Library

The library's use is intended for all people in the community; we've established that in previous chapters, and communities are diverse, so we're serving all kinds of people. It's incumbent upon the library to ensure that each member of the community is welcome in the library, can feel safe in the library, and has a sense of belonging in the library. Much can be done to ensure this. When thinking about children's departments, a good starting point is to take some time to survey existing spaces; in what ways do children feel that the space is for their use? Are books easily accessible? Physical space will be the first consideration. Next, I'll discuss the importance of equity, diversity, inclusion, and belonging in children's services along with a discussion of the importance of inclusivity, ensuring staff understand these topics and how outreach can benefit. Part of that diverse community includes folks who may need accommodations, so I'll explore space and program planning through that lens as well.

Jennifer Velásquez, in *Real-World Teen Services*, discusses teens' need for space, but this transfers in some ways to children's rooms as well. She states that "Space is power."[1] A simple but true statement. Children have the benefit of a long history of designated library space. Having that space clearly shows that the library invites kids, and kids, in turn, understand that they're welcome. Historically, the Carnegie model in libraries included both adult and children's spaces, so thinking back to the history of youth services in the first chapter, at least in Carnegie libraries and much more so today, kids know they can come to the library—that they have their own space.[2]

SPACE PLANNING

The first thing I think about when considering a children's room in a library is *color*. I know this isn't a critical or even the most important thing a library offers for youth, but for me, and for most people, walking into a space for the first time, the vibe sets the tone. Does it feel welcoming, bright, and cheerful, or is it grungy and neglected? Think it can't happen? I've had a first-hand experience. I moved back to New Hampshire in 1999, and the director of a nearby public library refused to purchase materials for teens because I was told in secret by a staff member that the director did not want teens in the library. Can you imagine? You must know that my heart broke upon hearing this, but I soon discovered as I stepped into the children's room that it was worse than I imagined. The books on the shelves were old with no out-facing books, just rows and rows of spine labels. The walls were not only dingy and white, but they were also dirty. There were a few bits of artwork on the walls, but they were too small for the space and were seriously outdated. It was awful. The physical space sent a strong message that the library didn't care about its young readers. In direct contrast and now under new management, the library has transformed. I recently visited that same children's room, and the change was palpable. Kids love coming to the library now—big soft chairs, color everywhere, a total reorganization of books, displays—the whole place just said, "We want children to visit the library! This space is for you!"

Your youth department space makes a huge difference in whether children will feel welcome or not. My best advice to you is this: In the same way that, when preparing for first-time guests in my home, I look at it through their eyes, survey your children's room through the eyes of a child. Are there toys? Is it colorful? Are books easy to access? Do you see book covers everywhere? Is the signage clear and fun? Is there seating for caregivers? I'll examine these space considerations and others in this section.

Thinking about the needs of children of different ages, you'll have to consider their level of independence and what needs they have. Toddlers will require a very different kind of space than middle schoolers. Toddlers need toys, soft areas to rest in, and books at their level as well as space for caregivers. Middle schoolers will require tables for homework and comfortable areas to hang out with their friends. Create a checklist for a self-assessment of various age groups, visit other libraries and then go back to your own. What does your library do well, and what needs improvement? This is just the beginning of working towards creating your welcoming and safe space for young readers.

DÉCOR AND COMFORT

As I mentioned earlier, the vibe of the children's room is important in making a first and lasting impression. If you're planning space in a new building or are lucky enough to be remodeling, then depending on budget, community needs, and staff considerations, you have more options and are working with a blank slate. Begin with a color scheme that works, and just like at home, you may prefer a more neutral palette with pops of color, or maybe every shade on the color wheel will be represented. If you're working with existing space and want to improve the look of the room, think about how color already works (or doesn't work) and consider your budget and what changes you're able to make. No budget at all? Look at signage and work on making that especially inviting with color and images. Also, think about what makes *you* feel comfortable and cozy; figure out how to implement that comfort in the children's room. Should you include oversized beanbag chairs? A couch? Soft furniture? Check out design schemes online and in person to explore the possibilities. Take a field trip to other libraries to experience their spaces in person; what elements can you bring back to your library? Ask the librarians where you've toured how they designed or improved their space; they may have some ideas that you can implement.

A very quick search on Pinterest yielded some amazing ideas for inspiring children's rooms. From a dinosaur that appears to be busting through the ceiling to a massive open book "roof" over the kid's area to giant windmill seating, you'll find plenty of bright ideas here. These are clearly libraries with expansive budgets, but by adapting some of these concepts, even those with the smallest budget can transform the space into something exciting. One idea I thought was clever was creating a tree from paper that enveloped a doorway, the canopy expanding upward with the trunk wrapping around the sides of the door. I even discovered a full-size Volkswagen van modified to fit under a bank of windows to provide a reading "room."[3] The possibilities are endless.

Your space for the children's department may be limited, so ensuring that you have movable furniture to transform areas for multiple uses just makes good sense. Our youth staff in Rye, with the help of a few volunteers, can transform the collection area into an open performance space in about fifteen minutes. Helpful caregivers and librarians have become very familiar with the routine of moving all our stacks out of the children's area and opening the space for floor seating for children. Bookcases on wheels made this possible, so consider multiple-use concepts.

AGE-APPROPRIATE AREAS, SAFETY, AND ACCESSIBILITY

It only makes sense that the areas for children are "age-appropriate." You wouldn't include just adult furniture in the children's room; it doesn't fit their smaller stature, and it's likely not soft around the edges. Children need spaces to cuddle up and get cozy. The tables and chairs should be appropriately sized for use. In my library, years ago, someone purchased wooden chairs for the children's room. They look beautiful, but in fact, the way the legs are cut and sized encourages them to fall backward when children are in them! Danger! Be sure to check furniture and equipment for safety. Look around carefully to determine potential hazards and strategize options, whether that is to reorganize your furniture or to purchase new ones, recognizing that safety is first, but correct sizing, comfort, and durability are also important.

A functional children's room will provide accessibility for all—so the bookshelves and bins should be lower, and as mentioned, furniture should be sized properly, with toys and games placed in areas that can easily be reached by small children. Additionally, think about patrons with disabilities who need easy access to materials—are the aisles and doorways wide enough for a wheelchair? Whether the user is young or is a caretaker, maneuverability in the room should be evaluated. In the same way that materials should reflect an understanding of the needs of those with disabilities, such as large-print books, audiobooks, and braille options, space needs should allow for these users and their needs as well.

Finally, a good overview of planning spaces in the youth department can be found at Demco Interiors. Check out Stephen Gower, Angela Loewecke, and Amber Benesch's "Checklist: Designing Engaging Library Spaces for Children" at https://www.demcointeriors.com/blog/designing-library-spaces-for-children/.

MAKING THE SPACE INTERACTIVE

For younger children, provide interactive elements to engage them—a wooden train set, dollhouse, sensory table, giant floor-size puzzles, blocks—my library has included all these types of toys, and we rotate them to keep engagement fresh. Interactive displays can draw attention to young library users and provide further engagement; every summer, I solicited help from the library director, a graphic designer and an amazing artist, to create a cardboard cutout photo op related to the theme of the reading program. Kids loved this. Voting jars were a big hit—place a voting jar under photos of several characters in a book and have kids put a token in the jar to vote for their favorite character. Guessing jars are always fun; we included one every summer, with the winner taking a full jar of gummies home that matched the theme of the reading program. I recently viewed a student's work who planned a guessing jar not just once per year but opted for one each month of the year; she was very creative with jar contents matching the monthly theme.

EQUITY, DIVERSITY, INCLUSION AND BELONGING: CREATING SAFE SPACE WITHIN CHILDREN'S SERVICES

I have another story to start this section; in the spring of 2016, I was invited to serve on a panel for the New Hampshire Library Association's Young Adult Library Services one-day conference. The focus was LGBTQIA2S+ teens, and since I had focused much of my graduate work on the topic and subsequently made library services to LGBTQIA2S+ teens one of my main career focus areas, I was delighted to be invited. Although some of the details are lost, what I distinctly remember was when a fellow panelist made a statement that, well, times have changed, and LGBTQIA2S+ teens were no longer facing the difficulties they had in the past. Initially, I was dumbfounded and then quickly apoplectic . . . mostly just seriously angry. At the time, I was writing a book on library services for queer teens, and I consistently discovered stories about hate crimes that included vicious attacks on this vulnerable group. I didn't have to look far; I only had to turn on the TV, read news stories, or do basic research. As I write this, the anger towards and targeting of the LGBTQIA2S+ community is growing to untenable proportions; a Human Rights Campaign February 15, 2023, press release headline reads, "Human Rights Campaign Working to Defeat 340 Anti-LGBTQ+ Bills at State Level Already, 150 of which Target Transgender People—Highest Number on Record."[4]

I know as a member of the LGBTQIA2S+ myself, I felt such a relief when I learned I was able to legally marry my lifelong partner. I was in a San Francisco hotel room prepping for my day at the ALA Conference when I caught the news. I sat down and wept. For a person of my age to finally see recognition and acceptance was paramount, a relief; honestly, the feelings are bigger than words can adequately describe. For children who are trying to understand their own identity, finding their place in the world when hate crimes are all too common is absolutely frightening. As I will repeat frequently in this section, libraries are one of the few places where vulnerable populations can have a sense of safety; representation on the shelves with the presence of inclusive titles ensures that people are welcome.

These statistics only include issues facing LGBTQIA2S+ folks; racial and religious targeting is rampant as well. In March of 2023, the FBI released 2021 hate crime statistics. As reported by Reuters, "The FBI said reported hate crime incidents rose to 9,065 in 2021 from 8,120 in 2020. The bureau said 64.5% of hate crime victims in 2021 were targeted because of their race, ethnicity or ancestry bias, while 15.9% were targeted because of sexual-orientation and 14.1% due to religion."[5] We can say times are rough, even worse than we imagined, but numbers are cold and sterile as they do not reflect the daily angst of family members, neighbors, and other vulnerable community members—the individuals represented by these numbers.

The statistical foundation mentioned is provided to help illustrate that, yes, in fact, there are many people for whom the library is essential. Censorship attempts and other legislation limiting the library's ability to include diverse titles are occurring at an alarming rate all around the country, but many libraries are holding the course and fighting back in the name of intellectual freedom. More on this later, but the key here is that the library plays a significant role in providing youth with resources and permitting minority groups to find stories like theirs on the shelves. Representation matters. A lot. As I outlined in *Serving LGBTQ Teens: A Practical Guide for Librarians*, taking the time to ensure representation for the LGBTQIA2S+ population "may very well save someone's life. This may seem like a wild exaggeration, but in fact, it's quite true. Story after story of teens who have been bullied, outcast, ejected from their own families for being queer still abound today. These young and vulnerable youth are commonly part of the homeless population and at serious risk for any number of life-threatening situations, including suicide. While that is a grim reality, it's also true that many LGBTQ teens in these situations have found refuge in the library—historically, public libraries function as 'safe havens"[6]

Much of this discussion centers around teens, but just as importantly, applying this to children's services, by including all kinds of families and children shows the library is welcoming.

DIVERSE REPRESENTATION

As I've stressed many times now, representation matters. Time and again, my students who are required to read widely in both children and teen literature for assignments remark that they wish they'd had books like the ones they're encountering now when they were children. I read often of folks who always thought they were uniquely alone in their feelings of alienation being opened to a world of diverse literature and finding their place and knowing they are not alone. A measure of this was mentioned in the last section, but the library is specially charged with ensuring that all members of the community are adequately represented in all areas.

The collection is an obvious place to start, but remember to include graphic novels, audiobooks, e-books, Playaways, and, really, any materials you include in your children's room. Kelsey Bogan mentions that not only does the library need representation in these areas, but it also needs to ensure that within genres, there is also adequate representation: realistic fiction, fantasy, mystery, thriller, and so on. And she points out, don't just settle for representation—it needs to be GOOD representation. Bogan notes, and the capitalization is Bogan's, though Bogan's original bolding is not present here: "It takes a lot of research, and it takes listening to readers and reviewers to tell the difference. And it means LISTENING TO PEOPLE OF COLOR AND LGBTQIA2S+ PEOPLE WHEN THEY TELL US THAT CERTAIN BOOKS ARE BAD REPRESENTATION AND ARE CAUSING HARM. And it means weeding those books."[7]

Speaking of representation and finding diverse works in the library, consider findability: How is the library cataloging these diverse books, what are current search words, and is there a method for evaluating and updating search words? Recent conversations in my library around subject headings have been illuminating. While I had learned much on the topic in library school, especially about the radical cataloging work of Sandy Berman, I only recently became aware of how troublesome search terms can be. On one hand, historical search terms that were used to categorize a book may now be insulting to some, and on the other hand, newer terms that might be substituted may not be recognized when searching for that same book. At a minimum, check out the Library of

Congress (LOC) bank of subject headings; are your records updated with these terms? While the LOC has made strides, the system for change is slow to keep up with current terminology. In 2016, the ALA issued a directive that, despite the LOC's inability to shift offensive terminology around undocumented people in the United States, libraries should adopt terminology anyway.[8] Along with issues of racism and bias inherent in the Dewey Decimal System, it's important to think about how you might remedy these problems. Take a deeper dive into the topics; they can be contentious, and you'll likely find heated arguments, but the real question is the following: If something is harming someone, why would the library endorse it? I'm still learning—in fact, an opening statement I make in all my courses is that I've committed to lifelong learning, and I don't claim to know it all! I do know that awareness leads to change. Make yourself aware, and let people know the library is for everyone—that all people are respected and heard. An excellent approach to beginning the process of adjusting troublesome terminology is to include a statement within the search area of your catalog mentioning that the library is working in earnest to adjust terminology and apologizes for any terms used or found that are offensive.

In addition to the collection, search terms, and the Dewey issues, Bogan also challenges librarians to think about signage, artwork, displays, and voices that are highlighted and not just during a respective celebration month but all the time.[9] Visually, the library should ensure that images and displays represent the community, and rotating the visuals will ensure you can. Ever think about a simple sign that reads, "If you like this book, then read. . . ." lists? Bogan reminds us that these lists should include representation, preferably with descriptions so that every patron recognizes library support toward all community members. It's not enough to display these materials just during, say, June for Pride Month or February for Black History Month. Finally, some sage advice: Work on your own "to-be-read" piles and lists, adding in new and classic diverse materials. Conduct a self-assessment and ask yourself the following: What are you reading to expand yourself beyond what you know?[10] To remain current is to actively seek out ways to grow towards cultural competence.

INCLUSIVE LANGUAGE, SENSITIVITY, RESPECT, AND ACCESSIBILITY

As with representation mentioned in this chapter, awareness of using inclusive language is needed. On those banners, book lists, displays, and signage, use language and imagery that includes a wide range of people. Staff should use inclusive language when speaking with patrons and should avoid making assumptions about gender, race, ethnicity, or other characteristics—including family dynamics. Don't assume the caregiver with a child is a biological parent. Inclusive language avoids using terms that discriminate against groups of people that show some kind of bias or include expressions that are not appropriate. Welcoming and honoring all people is the goal! Note that when you do make a mistake—we're only human—simply apologize, correct your error, and move on. No need to belabor your error—just keep focused on the person with whom you're interacting rather than making yourself and your apology the center of attention.

PROFESSIONAL DEVELOPMENT

Understanding, discussing, and addressing underlying biases, uncertainties, and even fears of religions, cultures, race, disabilities, sexual orientation, and the many things that make us "other" can be made safer through professionally guided discussions. Your library's attitude towards professional development and lifelong learning is the key to making the commitment in comprehending the notion of cultural humility and striving for cultural competence, which, in turn, creates an atmosphere of acceptance and ensures all people understand that they belong in the library. Recently, the staff at my library held a professional development session presented by James T. McKim, Jr., on "How to Have Difficult Conversations," and in it, he discusses the foundation needed to interact and discuss race in a meaningful way—one that is respectful, ensures listening and hearing, and uses basic relationship models. You can find his work at his company's website, organizationalignition.com, or read his book, *The Diversity Factor: Igniting Superior Organizational Performance*. Staff as a group, and staff individually, are responsible to seek out educational opportunities and strive for cultural competence. Search your local region for educational opportunities for yourself and your staff.

OUTREACH AND ENGAGEMENT

Develop relationships with partners in your community to increase cultural awareness and competence. Reach out to community LGBTQIA2S+ centers, PFLAG organizations, Native American Heritage Centers, African American Cultural Centers, NAACP Offices, ACLU offices, and Black Lives Matter organizations near you and determine how the library can support these organizations. Get creative with locating and connecting with these organizations and businesses in your area and listen to the needs of the community as you establish programming in the library to serve all people.

PROGRAMMING FOR CHILDREN WITH DISABILITIES

Aside from consideration of disabilities during space planning, more examination is called for to ensure appropriate access for all people. Note that the Americans with Disabilities Act of 1990 "requires facilities and services regularly used by the public to be accessible to the more than 43 million Americans who are physically or mentally disabled."[11] It's likely you know someone who has a visible disability, but not all disabilities are visible. In 2015, Denice Adkins and Bobbie Bushman noted that "The Census Bureau reports that 5.2 percent of school age (sic) children (2.8 million) were reported to have a disability. The American Community Survey defines a person with a disability as a person having a 'vision, hearing, cognitive, ambulatory, self-care, or independent living difficulty.' Per the American Community Survey, the most common type of disability diagnosed in school-age children is cognitive disability, which they define as 'serious difficulty concentrating, remembering, or making decisions.'"[12] Given this information, you may ask how you can make the library welcoming to all children, examine whether programs exclude children with disabilities in some way, and think about how any issues can be remedied effectively.

One area you can start with is the library's website; include links that support children with disabilities. San Francisco Public Library lists twelve links under People with Disabilities: Online and Walk-In Resources; see their site here at https://sfpl.org/locations/main-library/jobs-careers-center/jobs-and-careers-resources/resources-groups/people-disabilities. Specific tabs on their website are easy to locate and show the library's investment in providing inclusive service.

Since cognitive disabilities are the most common in youth, it is worth taking a moment to better understand what this means. According to the May Institute definition, "Developmental disabilities encompass a broad range of conditions that result from cognitive and/or physical impairments. They are identified before the age of 22, and usually last throughout a person's lifetime. These disabilities include intellectual disabilities, cerebral palsy, autism spectrum disorder, Down syndrome, language and learning disorders, vision impairment, and hearing loss."[13]

It is not within the scope of this book to examine all areas of cognitive disabilities, but a bit more depth in autism spectrum disorder and the use of the term "neurodiversity" is important. Avoid conflating the term neurodiversity with autism; Amelia Anderson states the term neurodiversity, coined in the 1990s by Judy Singer, "represents variations in the human brain . . . While autism is one form of neurodiversity, other neurological conditions or disorders such as attention deficit hyperactivity disorder (ADHD), dyslexia, and Tourette's syndrome also fall under the neurodiversity umbrella."[14] Note that Anderson's book, *Library Programming for Autistic Children and Teens*, 2nd Edition, is an excellent title for librarians interested in providing all age levels of programming for autistic children and teens as well as suggesting funding sources and training options.

ACCESSIBILITY: BEYOND THE ELEVATOR

Expounding a bit on previous space-planning considerations, specifically check your building to ensure access—are all areas accessible to people in wheelchairs? I know space constraints can make this challenging, and if this is the case, create signage showing the librarian's willingness to help people find what they're looking for. Be sure your signage is adequate by providing tools and assistive technology to help accommodate people with special needs. Since you may not be aware of all your patron's needs, you can start with some basics, such as creative signage highlighting the staff's willingness to assist.

Next, assess your assistive technologies and determine whether they're available for patrons who need them. My spouse is a land-use planner and has been working with communities in the Manchester, New Hampshire, region since 2016 on what she calls "becoming age friendly." She has found that librarians are very interested in this effort, even working on assessing libraries with an age-friendly filter. She shared a story about one of the libraries she had visited, where she was provided a facility tour that included a computer setup specifically for someone in a wheelchair. She took one look at the setup and pointed out to the librarian that a wheelchair could never fit under the desk. The setup had not been configured to the needed height and width. I share this story so that you consider your own space. One suggestion is to invite caregivers and youth with disabilities to assess the space for accessibility, signage, and tools.

To provide some examples of thoughtful design, at the New York Public Library, internet workstations are available to patrons needing screen-magnification software as well as screen-reading software; their Andrew Heiskell Braille and Talking Book Library offers even more software, including NVDA (nonvisual desktop access) screen-reading software; Talking Typing Teacher, for learning to type; Duxbury braille translation software; and Kurzweil 1000 scanning and reading software.[15] Additionally, various branches offer assistive amplification software, personal reading machines, and closed-circuit television enlargers.[16]

SENSORY SENSITIVITY

When planning programming for children with cognitive challenges, consider the environment itself. Comfort in these programs is paramount, so ensuring that all participants' needs are met is important. To determine that you are offering appropriate programming, check in with families who may be attending to assess any problems and ask that they provide suggestions. For example, ask how you can best create an atmosphere and physical space for a summer concert that may incorporate loud noises or bright lights. The solutions may be as simple as dimming the lights and using noise-canceling headphones. Show kids that it's okay to wear noise-canceling headphones by placing them on a large stuffed animal and reminding participants not everyone likes loud noises. Think about your five senses and how children may be impacted by noise, temperature, light, and even a large crowd of people, and adjust accordingly.

Be prepared for children with disabilities to respond uniquely to various situations. Noted by R. Lynn Baker, "Children who have sensory processing issues have difficulty receiving and interpreting information that is sent to their brains from their senses ... children may respond to sensory input in an unusual way, impacting their behavior, ability to listen, or social interactions with others."[17]

INCLUSIVITY

At some point in our lives, I imagine, we've all felt left out. It's a terrible feeling, and if it's repeated often, the feelings become deeply entrenched. Welcoming all children and making sure they know they're included is so very important. For instance, storytime for hearing children is commonplace, but what if, in addition to this storytime, you scheduled storytimes for non-hearing children; how about getting help from an ASL-proficient person who can sign at storytimes?

As with other groups of marginalized people, children with disabilities need to see themselves represented on the shelves—assess your children's room titles to determine how your collection measures up. Need help here? A quick Google search for books in the age range you're seeking along with the term "children with disabilities" will yield plenty—a recently posted site includes eight picture books featuring characters with disabilities; check out Al-Jadir's April 2022 section on the Disability Horizons website, Entertainment and Culture tab, and search "8 picture books" and you'll find the article.[18] In fact, explore the entire site at https://sfpl.org/locations/main-library/jobs-careers-center/jobs-and-careers-resources/resources-groups/people-disabilities.

Regarding collection development, it is likely you will want to not only research for great titles but also research reviews of those titles. I have discovered books that have been highly praised in their depiction of children with disabilities that, in fact, raise issues. As an example, I was very interested to read that a book I had enjoyed, *Rules*, by Cynthia Lord, creates issues around David, the autistic younger brother of Catherine, the story's protagonist; the titular rules are created to avoid Catherine's embarrassment, and she works hard to discourage David from these behaviors. Further, David's parents do not acknowledge his means of communication and prohibit Catherine from using his preferred method of communication.[19] Although this may provide a springboard for discussion, it also is important to utilize reviewers' insights to help you decide whether or not a book is for your collection or not.

Finally, hearkening back to those Library of Congress subject headings, educate yourself in accepted terminology and create a plan for how to address this in your catalog. A conversation with the library's cataloger will yield interesting results; if there isn't a designated cataloger in your library, seek out catalogers in libraries near you for a chat.

STAFF TRAINING

As with other areas around understanding the people we're serving in our libraries, staff training and awareness of the needs of children with disabilities will ensure they are equipped with the right tools to support children in the library. Understanding the challenges young people face forms the foundation for service. The May Institute notes that "The most common developmental disability is intellectual disability. Cerebral palsy is the second most common developmental disability, followed by autism spectrum disorder."[20] Gaining knowledge about these more common disabilities is a good place to start in staff education. One approach could be to set goals during staff evaluations and provide information about educational workshops and other professional development opportunities.

OUTREACH/PARTNERSHIPS

Once programming for children with disabilities is established, how does the library reach the families who need to know about them? Penny Peck outlines in her book *Crash Course in Children's Programming* the following great ideas for getting the word out:

- Library staff can visit children with special needs at their local schools and organizations. This includes visits to parenting groups to share what the library has to offer.
- Invite parents with a special needs child to be part of your library governing board.
- Partner with doctors, social service agencies, and others who serve families with children with special needs so they might distribute handouts and other publicity materials.
- Be sure to mention that children with special needs are welcome at your library, at storytime, and at your programs, and make this a regular part of your flyers and brochures.
- Add elements to your storytimes and program that accommodate these needs, such as reserved seating for those with disabilities, wheelchair seating, tactile elements at storytime, stay-and-play opportunities at storytime, and parenting sharing time after the program.
- Promote inclusion of those with special needs at all levels of the library by advocating for staff training.
- Check out the information on Disability Awareness Training from the Association of Library Service to Children, a division of the ALA: https://www.alsc.ala.org/blog/2013/05/disability-awareness-training-essential-tools-for-your-toolbox/.[21]

You might also consider including stuffed animals with disabilities in your displays. By making crutches, wheelchairs, noise-canceling headphones, and other assistive devices more commonplace, perhaps kids using them won't feel so self-conscious.

Search out organizations in your area that provide support for children with disabilities. By reaching out to organizations who specialize in supporting children with disabilities, the library can solicit guidance on best practices; in some cases, these organizations may even partner with the library to provide effective programming as well as providing staff with educational materials.

FEEDBACK

Before you implement programming for children with disabilities, survey your community to determine the need; you may benefit from feedback. Even if this call for feedback doesn't yield results, plan programming and see it through. You may be surprised by how much of a need you have in your community—families may be reluctant to speak out for their children to ensure their comfort, and they may prefer not to attend widely inclusive programming out of concern that their child's behavior may be disruptive.

Once you've held programming geared to children with specific needs, check in with attendees to determine what you've done right and identify areas that need improvement. Feedback like this should inform future program offerings.

It's my hope that every person seeking library services is welcome in the library, has his, her, or their needs met, and finds materials that mirror themselves. Thoughtful planning, persistent research, and a desire to understand your community all serve to raise that library to an exceptional status level.

REVIEW QUESTIONS

1. Explore the children's space in the library where you currently work or visit a local library and evaluate: Is it welcoming? Is it comfortable? Is it safe? Are there interactive elements for children to explore? What do you observe related to signage related to welcoming all people?
2. Why is it important for all people to be represented on library shelves? Research this question further and report on your findings.
3. As in the first question, examine the children's department for visible signs of welcome for children with disabilities. Does the library offer programming directed to those children and their families?
4. Identify several organizations in your local area that might offer partnerships related to diversity and children who have disabilities.

NOTES

1. Jennifer Velásquez, *Real-World Teen Services* (Chicago: ALA Editions, 2015), 2.
2. Ibid., 4.
3. Pinterest: Becky Isbell, "Awesome Children's Library Inspiration," accessed May 12, 2023, https://www.pinterest.com/pin/43487952633131860/.
4. HRC Staff, "Human Rights Campaign Working to Defeat 340 Anti-LGBTQIA2S+ Bills at State Level Already, 150 of which Target Transgender People—Highest Number on Record," accessed May 12, 2023, https://www.hrc.org/press-releases/human-rights-campaign-working-to-defeat-340-anti-LGBTQIA2S+-bills-at-state-level-already-150-of-which-target-transgender-people-highest-number-on-record.
5. Sarah N. Lynch, "Hate crimes in US surged 11.6% in 2021, fueled by racial, ethnic bias," accessed May 12, 2023, https://www.reuters.com/world/us/hate-crimes-us-surged-116-2021-2023-03-13/.
6. Lisa Houde, *Serving LGBTQ Teens: A Practical Guide for Librarians* (Lanham, MD: Rowman & Littlefield, 2018), 1.
7. Kelsey Bogan, "Developing a Library that's REALLY for Everyone," accessed May 12, 2023, https://dontyoushushme.com/2021/03/02/__trashed/.
8. American Library Association, "ALA Welcomes Removal of Offensive 'Illegal Aliens' Subject Headings," accessed May 26, 2023, https://www.ala.org/news/member-news/2021/11/ala-welcomes-removal-offensive-illegal-aliens-subject-headings.
9. Bogan, "Developing a Library that's REALLY for Everyone."
10. Ibid.
11. Colorin' Colorado, "Library Services for Children with Special Needs," accessed May 13, 2023, https://www.colorincolorado.org/article/library-services-children-special-needs.
12. Denice Adkins and Bobbie Bushman, "A Special Needs Approach: A Study of How Libraries Can Start Programs for Children with Disabilities," *Children & Libraries: The Journal of the Association for Library Service to Children* 13, no. 3 (2015): 28. doi:10.5860/cal.13n3.28.
13. The May Institute, "Developmental Disabilities," accessed May 13, 2023, https://www.mayinstitute.org/autism-aba/developmental-disabilities.html.
14. Amelia Anderson, *Library Programming for Autistic Children and Teens*, 2nd Edition (Chicago: ALA Editions, 2021), 11.
15. New York Public Library, "Assistive Technologies," accessed May 13, 2023, https://www.nypl.org/node/7005.
16. New York Public Library, "Other Assistive Technologies," accessed May 13, 2023, https://www.nypl.org/node/88.
17. R. Lynn Baker, *Creating Literacy-Based Program for Children: Lesson Plans and Printable Resources for K-5* (Chicago: ALA Editions, 2015).
18. Disability Horizons, "8 Children's Books with Disabled Characters," accessed May 13, 2023, https://disabilityhorizons.com/2022/04/8-childrens-books-with-disabled-characters/.
19. Anderson, *Library Programming for Autistic Children and Teens*, 2nd Edition, 11.
20. The May Institute, "Developmental Disabilities."
21. Penny Peck, *Crash Course in Children's Services*, 2nd Edition (Santa Barbara, CA: Libraries Unlimited, 2014).

7

Intellectual Freedom, Censorship, and Professional Ethics

This chapter focuses on some challenging issues. Daily news includes stories of books being challenged, banned, and, sometimes, even burned. Harsh laws are being enacted to punish librarians for providing what some consider "harmful" materials. Librarians, however, have a professional duty to ensure the collection includes materials for all people, providing them access to materials from which they might benefit. The issues are hotly debated and complex, and in many circumstances, there are no easy answers. What follows in this chapter is an overview of intellectual freedom and censorship, a further exploration of self-censorship, and foundations in professional ethics.

INTELLECTUAL FREEDOM: CRITICAL TO LIBRARY SERVICES

Let's get to some basic definitions. I'll start with intellectual freedom itself and why it's important. Wikipedia offers this: "Intellectual freedom encompasses the freedom to hold, receive and disseminate ideas without restriction. Viewed as an integral component of a democratic society, intellectual freedom protects an individual's right to access, explore, consider, and express ideas and information as the basis for a self-governing, well-informed citizenry. Intellectual freedom comprises the bedrock for freedoms of expression, speech, and the press and relates to freedoms of information and the right to privacy."[1] This is a good definition, and along with that, the Wikipedia site offers decent foundational information that includes the court cases that form the history of intellectual freedom. If you're able, though, purchase the ALA's *Intellectual Freedom Manual*, which outlines so much more as it relates directly to librarianship.

It is incumbent upon librarians to uphold the precepts of intellectual freedom and ensure access to materials for all patrons—and this means even those materials that don't align with the librarian's personal beliefs and opinions. Checking the ALA website, you'll find professional ethics admonitions around this topic—especially as it relates to First Amendment Rights. Explore the First Amendment, privacy laws, and intellectual property rights for a well-rounded knowledge base. A search in Google for these terms will direct your exploration, but always check the ALA website for information relating directly to librarianship.

One excellent resource printed by ALA's Office for Intellectual Freedom, and mentioned earlier, is the *Intellectual Freedom Manual*. Now in its tenth edition, the book cannot be disputed as the ultimate resource in these matters; my library and personal copies are well-thumbed with a rainbow of sticky notes throughout. There's so much to explore here, but you'll find five steps to take in your library right out of the gate—first page—then in three parts, every aspect of intellectual freedom and censorship is provided in detail. You'll even find a full section focused on children and youth. Another title that has been useful in my library work is Emily Knox's 2022 title *Foundations of Intellectual Freedom*.[2] Knox includes historical information on intellectual freedom as well as placing it squarely in 2022 as the concept relates to current events. Each chapter is highly readable and includes discussion questions as well as further reading suggestions.

DEFINING BANNING AND CENSORSHIP

Banning library materials is the result of a successful challenge. A person attempts to challenge a book, for example, and if they are successful, it will be removed from the library; the distinction is important as the terms are not interchangeable. Banning is equivalent to censorship.

Censorship is the active prohibition of access to books, movies, magazines, or other materials. As noted by the ACLU, "Censorship, the suppression of words, images, or ideas that are 'offensive,' happens whenever some people succeed in imposing their personal political or moral values on others. Censorship can be carried out by the government as well as private pressure groups. Censorship by the government is unconstitutional."[3]

The issue here is that people who object to materials in the library seek to limit access to that material for ALL people. I can't help but echo what I've heard over the years that I've been in the library—if you don't like a book, don't read it—just don't decide that other people shouldn't read it either. I came across a meme recently that read, and I'm paraphrasing: Steps to take when you'd like to have a book removed from the library: Step 1. Read a different book. Makes sense to me!

AWARENESS OF CHALLENGES

A simple search in Google will yield more information than you could take in about challenges in today's contentious climate. Read current articles on the topic and search ALA's website for the most challenged books lists. Understand trends in what people are seeking to exclude from the library's collection, or even those that folks think should be moved, say, from the young adult department to the adult department. Get smart about what's going on and this will prepare you for such potential issues in your library. I encourage you to read these banned and challenged books—not just during banned books week but, instead, all year! As of this writing, note that of the top thirteen titles most challenged in 2022, seven of those cited LGBTQIA2S+ issues as the reasons.

I've observed and have seen others question the logic behind these challenges. Yes, sometimes they end up being removed from library shelves, but more often, just calling out the title as something to be censored makes them more attractive to youth—am I right about this? This happened with Pulitzer Prize-winning *Maus* by Art Spiegelman when a Tennessee school board banned the book; the title was in such demand that Amazon noted there may not be copies available to meet orders.[4]

Back in the old days, bound copies listing books with reasons for challenges were produced, which I dutifully purchased every year; accessing this information on the ALA's website is much easier.

I need to end this section with some good advice for kids in relation to banning and challenging books; it's a quote from Stephen King that I've seen on Goodreads that states, "Yet when books are run out of school classrooms and even out of school libraries as a result of this idea, I'm never much disturbed not as a citizen, not as a writer, not even as a schoolteacher ... which I used to be. What I tell kids is, don't get mad, get even. Don't spend time waving signs or carrying petitions around the neighborhood. Instead, run, don't walk, to the nearest non-school library or to the local bookstore and get whatever it was that they banned. Read whatever they're trying to keep out of your eyes and your brain, because that's exactly what you need to know."[5]

SELF-CENSORSHIP

Guilty! I'm afraid to admit that I was among those who practiced self-censorship—without even knowing it. I mentioned this story in a previous chapter of this book, but it bears repeating in this area dedicated to the concept of self-censorship. When I first began my library career in the youth department, I was fresh out of teaching English at a Catholic school. There, any titles I included in my classroom met the strict guidelines of adhering to the Catholic Church's precepts. I became used to "protecting" kids and ensuring they weren't exposed to any literature that included what may be considered objectionable by the Church.

This was a deeply entrenched principle I held while teaching at that school. In the public library, spillover was evident when I read, with great alarm over the disturbing content, *Living Dead Girl*, by Elizabeth Scott. I reluctantly cataloged the book, but rather than displaying it as "new," I shelved it. I hang my head in shame. I've learned so much, and Debra Whelan, in her article "A Dirty Little Secret: Self-Censorship is Rampant and Lethal," outlines author Barry Lyga's strange situation over his book *Boy Toy*, published in 2007. Expecting backlash over its publication due to a sexual encounter between a twelve-year-old boy and his teacher, the backlash never came. Bookstores and libraries were quietly keeping the books off the shelves despite its incredible reviews and many of those adults—librarians and booksellers—who had read it, had loved it. "'It's sort of a soft, quiet, very insidious censorship, where nobody is raising a stink, nobody is complaining, nobody is burning books,' says Lyga about the plight of *Boy Toy*. 'They're just quietly making sure it doesn't get out there.'"[6]

Today, self-censorship is rampant, not only for the reasons I had experienced in the early days of my library career and were briefly mentioned in a previous chapter, but also because there's a new legitimate fear; librarians fear losing their jobs, facing fiercely angry objections to books, and even breaking the law and facing prison. Think this is hyperbole? As of May of 2023, five states have adopted laws in which librarians face exorbitant fines or prison time for permitting minors access to "harmful" or "sexually explicit" material; as of this writing, nine states have similar laws pending, two states have vetoed laws, and four states have defeated similar laws.[7]

While I've included references to young adult literature and censorship, literature for middle grades and children face challenges as well. As of February of 2022, Nikki lists thirteen middle-grade books that were challenged: *George, Bridge to Terabithia, The Amulet of Samarkand, The Supernaturalist, New Kid, Olive's Ocean, Totally Joe, Anne Frank: The Diary of a Young Girl, Drama, Better Nate Than Never*, the Harry Potter book set, *l8r, g8r*, and *White Bird*.[8] According to Pen America's Lisa Tolin, nineteen picture books were among the most banned for the 2021-2022 school year. They were: *Pride: The Story of Harvey Milk and the Rainbow Flag, I am Jazz, And Tango Makes Three, In Our Mothers' House, The Baby Tree, Separate is Never Equal, Everywhere Babies, Worm Loves Worm, When Aiden Became a Brother, We March, We are Grateful, They, She, He Easy as ABC, The Name Jar, The Family Book, Sulwe, Stella Brings the Family, Sparkle Boy, Sing a Song*, and *Radiant Child: The Story of Young Artist Jean-Michel Basquiat*.[9] From the titles listed here, hot-button issues are clearly focused on LGBTQ content and titles relating to race.

Final thoughts on this topic that helped me understand why books with challenging topics and scenarios belong on the shelf come from a teen. This teen consumed what's considered by some to be "harmful"; she especially devoured titles written by Ellen Hoskin in record numbers. In a conversation, I casually asked her what the appeal was. She told me that these books helped her to see her own life through a different lens—helping her realize that she was okay and that her life was going along just fine in comparison to what she was reading. That perspective is but one reason teens need these books; ultimately, despite the harshness of the situations and material, teens are experiencing many horrors themselves. They deserve access to books that may help them work through their issues so they know that they're not alone.

This is grim news, but I'd like to end this section with some hopeful words from Pat Scales, a celebrated librarian whose passion is intellectual freedom. The *School Library Journal* piece in her "On Censorship" column of January 11, 2024, lists questions from librarians and features Pat's responses. Ultimately, Pat is hopeful for the future of intellectual freedom. She notes several instances in which censored books are being reinstated, book clubs reading banned books are being formed, and students are taking up the cause for the freedom to read; she states, "Am I hopeful? Yes, because I believe in young people. They will get the job done if we nudge them along."[10]

POLICIES AND PROCEDURES

Discussed in part in the collection development section, it's worth restating that the library's ability to protect intellectual freedom rights finds its foundation in the collection development and weeding policies, and this should include not only the reconsideration policy but also verbiage around where a title is housed—in the young adult section, in the middle grade section, and so on.

Staff training in how to communicate effectively with those who wish to challenge titles in the library is a must. Research this topic and share your findings with staff to help them in potentially difficult and upsetting situations. I was personally enlightened when reading James LaRue's *A New Inquisition: Understanding and Managing Intellectual Freedom Challenges*. Chapter 4, "Responding to Challenges," was especially helpful with potential face-to-face encounters; I had the chance to enact what I read there and can vouch for its efficacy. A patron was deeply distressed about a display in the young adult room and became quite agitated in her conversation with me; rather than "pick up the rope" and defend the display, I merely listened and repeated back what I was hearing the person say from time to time. By the end of the conversation, the patron thanked me for listening and no official challenge was made. As LaRue states, most folks just want to express their concerns and go no further; if they feel they've been heard, that may be enough for them, and no formal complaint will be lodged.[11] LaRue's title was published in 2007, but it is still relevant today. Lucky for me, this was as far as the complaint went; today's climate sees a different kind of contentiousness, but despite this, the tools outlined by LaRue can and do work well.

I was so enamored of the practical approach offered by LaRue, expressed far more eloquently and in-depth than my meager offering here, that I contacted him to let him know this, and requested that he become a guest speaker in a course I teach at San José State University every semester; I'm delighted to report that he accepted and has been a favorite guest speaker of my students in Materials for Young Adults every semester since. I highly recommend this title for all librarians! I cannot state this strongly enough.

PROFESSIONAL ETHICS

I've come to learn much about exactly how my work as a librarian is shaped and defined by the ethical considerations that inform that work. I had something of an uphill climb, as I noted in the anecdote earlier, especially around self-censorship. A careful reading of the American Library Association's Code of Ethics provides clear guidance. You'll likely have been doing your work according to these guidelines without necessarily articulating them as outlined in ALA's professional code, as many things are common sense. Helping patrons the best you're able and keeping and upholding intellectual freedom precepts are two of the many codes listed in the Code of Ethics.[12] Review this site from time to time as a reminder or visit it for the first time to educate yourself; it encapsulates the foundational facets of library work. The list can be found here: https://www.ala.org/tools/ethics.

I admit to being overwhelmed by the challenges to intellectual freedom and the daily news of censorship attempts, hearing about librarians having to fight to retain their jobs, and the outrageous and sometimes violent behaviors being exhibited by those who wish to remove the freedom to read from others. I find hope in youth—that they'll make things right as we all fight to uphold the basic foundations of libraries.

REVIEW QUESTIONS

1. Examine precepts around professional ethics and explain the librarian's role in upholding intellectual freedom.
2. Seek out LaRue's *A New Inquisition: Understanding and Managing Intellectual Freedom Challenges.* Outline concepts that you've either employed or plan to adopt and mention any portions of chapter 4, especially, that have surprised or enlightened you.
3. Check out the most recent Pat Scales piece in *School Library Journal* from her On Censorship column; explore the concepts in the piece more deeply with research. Report on your findings.
4. Explore the most recent news on librarians facing fines and imprisonment; what has changed from the writing of this chapter? Discuss the updated information and determine whether progress is being made.

5. Find at least two examples of youth taking up the charge for the freedom to read. Report on your findings.
6. Read the ALA's Professional Ethics/Code of Ethics. Outline whether these concepts are ones that you've already espoused as well as mentioning new ideas you've encountered.

NOTES

1. Wikipedia, "Intellectual Freedom," accessed May 13, 2023, https://en.wikipedia.org/wiki/Intellectual_freedom.
2. Emily J. M. Knox, *Foundations of Intellectual Freedom* (Chicago: ALA Neal-Schuman, 2022).
3. ACLU, "What is Censorship?" accessed May 13, 2023, https://www.aclu.org/other/what-censorship.
4. Lee Brown, "Holocaust Book 'Maus' Sales Soar After School Board Ban," *New York Post*, accessed January 31, 2022, https://nypost.com/2022/01/31/holocaust-book-maus-sees-sales-soar-after-school-board-ban/.
5. Goodreads, "Stephen King-Quotes-Quotable Quotes," accessed January 29, 2024, https://www.goodreads.com/quotes/7347192-censorship-and-the-suppression-of-reading-materials-are-rarely-about.
6. Debra Whelan, "A Dirty Little Secret: Self-Censorship is Rampant and Lethal," *School Library Journal*, accessed January 29, 2024, https://www.slj.com/story/a-dirty-little-secret-self-censorship.
7. James Gordon, "Mapped: The U.S. states where school librarians face years in prison and tens of THOUSANDS in fines for providing 'harmful' books for children," *The Daily Mail*, accessed January 29, 2024, https://www.dailymail.co.uk/news/article-12109483/States-school-librarians-face-years-prison-tens-THOUSANDS-fines-harmful-books-children.html.
8. Nikki, "Middle Grade Reads: 13 Most Challenged & Banned Middle Grade Books," accessed January 30, 2024, https://middlegradereads.com/challenged-banned-books-middle-school/.
9. Lisa Tolin, "The Most Banned Picture Books of the 2021-2022 School Year," accessed January 30, 2024, https://pen.org/banned-picture-books-2022/.
10. Pat Scales, "How I Stay Hopeful About the Future of Free Speech | Scales on Censorship," *School Library Journal*, accessed January 29, 2024, https://www.schoollibraryjournal.com/story/how-I-stay-hopeful-about-the-future-of-free-speech-scales-on-censorship.
11. James LaRue, *The New Inquisition: Understanding and Managing Intellectual Freedom Challenges* (Westport, CT: Libraries Unlimited, 2007), 76.
12. American Library Association, "Code of Ethics," accessed February 7, 2024, https://www.ala.org/tools/ethics.

8

Foundations in Administration of Children's Services and Professional Development

"We will promote the value of reading and encourage the quest for knowledge and experience to enrich lifelong learning, discovery, and creativity."[1] Lifelong learners—notice that part? This is a section of the mission statement of the Rye Public Library in New Hampshire, and I believe many library's goals include lifelong learning. The goal of the library is to encourage and enrich lifelong learning in our patrons, but to do that effectively, librarians themselves must embrace their profession as a lifelong learner. It only makes sense, right?

A librarian's career may last decades, and during that time, multiple advances and changes in technology will occur. Procedural aspects of work will shift—cataloging, administrative operations, and other policies will invariably change—and they should. Change can be challenging, and I've worked with some people who have staunchly resisted change, particularly technological advancements, but to serve today's patrons, the librarian must be adept, flexible, and willing to embrace new approaches. To put it one way, a seeming mountain of change can be flattened to reasonable hills with a positive attitude and perseverance.

In this chapter, I'll be looking at librarianship through an administrative lens, and in all areas, the librarian is charged with embracing learning, seeking out discovery of new ideas, and creatively effecting change for today's library users and their unique needs. Specifically, the areas I'll cover here are core competencies for children's librarians, children's services advocacy, digital preparedness for children's librarians, management and leadership, outreach and marketing, and, finally, professional development.

CORE COMPETENCIES FOR YOUTH LIBRARIANS

Thinking about foundational elements of librarianship relating to children's services, the name that continued to appear time and again during my graduate school years, and indeed during the research for this book, is 2019 California Library Hall inductee Virginia Walter. I can think of no better place to start than Walter's five laws of children's librarianship—concepts that have stood the test of time. Walter based her five laws on Ranganathan's five laws of librarianship established in 1931, and they are:

1. Libraries serve the reading interests and information needs of all children, directly and through service to parents and other adults who are involved with the lives of children.
2. Children's librarians provide the right book or information for the right child at the right time in the right place.
3. Children's librarians are advocates for children's access to books, information, information technology, and ideas.
4. Children's librarians promote children's literacy in all media.
5. Children's librarians honor their traditions and create the future.[2]

It's quite neat to summarize the complexity of children's services in five laws, but each of these areas includes multi-pronged practices and theories. In fact, these blossom beautifully into the American Library Association's Association for Library Service to Children (ALSC) Competencies for Librarians Serving Children in Libraries. The competencies are outlined in Walter's book and can be found in nearly every title published for children's librarians. The ALSC updated the competencies in 2020, and you can find the most recent version on the ALSC website here: https://www.ala.org/alsc/edcareeers/alsccorecomps.

From my own experience and years of youth librarianship, it's no surprise that the first critical component of expert youth librarianship is to know the library patrons, and in children's services, that includes both children and their caregivers. At least a cursory understanding of children's developmental stages and needs should be included in the librarian's self-education. To offer age-appropriate services and programs, knowledge of age is critical. I found Karis Loop's division of ages in *Seamless Youth Services for Every Age and Stage* to be helpful. These include three areas within the storytime age, what Loop terms "The Vanishing Time," which encompasses storytime to school-age children. She also outlines the school-age spectrum, which leads directly into middle grades.[3] What I found most helpful about Loop's approach is the concept of "inching up the ramp" in which transitional times are addressed as much as major age divisions. Transitional programming is defined by Loop as "programs... that are meant to assist children as they move from one youth service stage to the next. Some of these transitional periods are major ones, including the large steps from storytimes to school-age programs."[4]

Before I leave this section and Loop's work, the three areas that are addressed in the book include the following competencies for each age level and the transitional periods: "how to self-select books, how to participate in programs, and how to use the library's resources."[5] To achieve those goals, Loop includes excellent suggestions for programs; check out the offerings in her book—you won't be disappointed!

The entirety of this chapter focuses on the elements of administration and management in children's services, so it's no wonder the ALSC includes these two areas as a competency for children's services.

In all the years I've worked in youth librarianship, and as the third of the competencies indicates, communication is paramount. Clear directives, clear goals, and excellent interpersonal skills—both written and verbal—help create a smoothly running department. In addition to this directive to communicate clearly with colleagues, patrons and their caregivers, and community members, one must also listen—listen to the needs of patrons, as well as to the needs and ideas of staff and colleagues. A key element of a good listener—and I've learned this from personal relationships, interactions with patrons, and even through LaRue's advice on interacting with patrons who may be filing a complaint—is repeating back and affirming what you've heard verbally. LaRue's book *A New Inquisition*, especially chapter 4, is extremely helpful on the topic of interacting with a patron filing a complaint; following his advice may help avoid the pitfalls of misunderstandings.

Whether talking with one patron or speaking in front of a group of caregivers and children to introduce a program, practice helps. When I transitioned from teaching junior high to working as a youth librarian; communicating with a large group of people was not an issue; remember, I taught young teens! Still, talking in front of a group, no matter how small, may seem daunting, but over time, practice and often encouragement from the children will help you become more comfortable.

Rounding out this section, written communication, effective reference interviews with both children and caregivers, and knowledge of library policies and procedures, along with the ability to articulate them to patrons, is important. These areas have been addressed in more depth in other chapters but bear mentioning here.

My dad sometimes calls me when I'm at the library, and he typically jokes, "Are you reading a good book?" I wish I had the time to read at work! Keeping up with current reading trends along with knowledge of current online offerings through the library is an important part of the work. Also, make it a goal to understand what various ages of kids are watching on streaming services, the video games, and other educational platforms they're playing on, and even the podcasts or music they may be listening to. As mentioned, I teach a Materials for Young Adults course at San José State University, and knowledge of these offerings is featured at the teen level in that class along with collection development advice, which includes consulting both formal and informal resources: *School Library Journal*, *Horn Book Magazine*, online blogs, and top ten books for kids. To remain current, search the terms "top 10 books for children 2023 October," as an example, for the latest popular titles. The *New York Times* bestseller list is a great resource, but also check on indie publishers and diversity blogs like "We Needs Diverse Books" to include a wide variety of titles and electronic offerings. Rounding out this area is the need for establishing criteria for materials acquisition and the librarian must also, according to ALSC, have a knowledge of cataloging or copy-cataloging according to current practices.

The reference interview, mentioned in an earlier chapter of this book, is a staple of the children's librarian's abilities in listening. Summarizing the remaining ALSC *Competencies for Librarians Service Children in Libraries*, all of which are addressed in more depth in this text, include the topics of advocacy, professional development, and technology.[6] For a more detailed outline of each area, check out the ALSC competencies online.

CHILDREN'S SERVICES ADVOCACY

Call it shameless self-promotion, call it beating your own drum, call it marketing; children's services advocacy can be all three. Effective advocacy requires promoting your work with children by ensuring that the library administration understands your needs, the public is participating in programs, and colleagues in the library know the work you're doing. Understanding the components of advocacy is critical to sustaining staff, resources, and patrons, so what, really, is advocacy? Though a basic dictionary definition may get the job done, I prefer The Alliance for Justice's definition, which is a bit more expansive: "Advocacy is defined as any action that speaks in favor of, recommends, argues for a cause, supports or defends, or pleads on behalf of others."[7] Sounds like a good fit for a library advocate to me!

A starting point outlined by Houde in *Public Libraries and Their Communities* by Kay Ann Cassell notes that the first place to employ shameless self-promotion involves buy-in from library administration.[8] Let your supervisors know your plans, and get them excited about new programs based on statistics and verbal feedback from young patrons. As mentioned in a previous chapter, embracing the plan in *5 Steps of Outcome-Based Planning and Evaluation* by Melissa Gross, Cindy Mediavilla, and Virgina A. Walters[9] will provide excellent statistics, performance measures, and anecdotes to support your work in the youth department.

Ensuring that the library community also knows what's happening in the library is vital, as illustrated by Cecilia Freda's statement in *Promoting Your Library: Getting the Message Out*: "What makes libraries particularly primed for advocacy is that so much of what goes on in them is invisible to the public eye. If our public thinks that circulating books is all we do and all that we must do, then how can we expect them to be impressed by our influence within the school community?"[10] While this example pertains to the school library, it applies just as easily to the work of the public library.

Brag about your work shamelessly! This is often difficult as it does sound like bragging, but outlining your accomplishments lets stakeholders know that there is good work being done and you're doing it! Consider sharing your work with this framework: "I'm so excited about a program we hosted last week—kids were engaged (be specific about how) and were asking for more; the staff and I were thrilled that our concept was so well received." See? This is a nice way of sharing your good work. This kind of "bragging" should be shared with stakeholders like the Friends of the Library group, library administration, Library Board of Trustees (if applicable), town or city administrators, patrons (taxpayers), and library colleagues. As you enthusiastically share your work, be sure to include your staff as having done well in the program—in other words, always give credit where credit is due! I referenced this back in chapter 5, and I'm repeating it here—it's just that important.

Lesley Farmer, in *Impactful Community-Based Literacy Projects*, clearly states that communication around projects is essential to maximize potential impacts: "To be impactful, literacy projects require regular and effective communication within and across each sector as well as to the community. The literacy project needs to be explained to its planners and implementers, partners, stakeholders, and the community at large to create awareness, interest, and support."[11]

In addition to advocating for your programming, you may find yourself needing to make a case for essential materials required for that programming. While it's not as common with children's services as it sometimes can be with young adult services, there are times when stakeholders may require further information around why specific programs and perhaps materials required for those programs are needed. Be ready to substantiate your plans with time-tested and research-supported statistics. There may be questions about why a sensory play program is needed due to the cost of materials; here, your understanding of childhood development will come into play.

One of my favorite advocacy tips comes from a 2020 piece in *Children and Libraries* by Erica Ruscio entitled "Everyday Advocacy: Doing What You Do." This short article encapsulates the value of advocacy in the youth department and mentions ALSC's *Championing Children's Services Toolkit*. Available online at no cost and easily found by searching the above title, this toolkit is wonderful—offering ideas I've never considered that, according to the article, provide a corresponding program idea with supportive background on why the programming is vital. Two examples are provided here, but the toolkit itself offers eight "reasons." The first in Ruscio's article is a program idea that addresses this concept: *Because Storytime is a Key Building Block to School Success* offers a program that invites stakeholders (Friends of the Library, Board of Trustees, the Public, etc.) to either observe a storytime session, or participate in one. I love this! The second corresponding program idea is to look for ways to showcase the work you're doing for stakeholders. What is the answer? *Because Libraries are Constantly Evolving.*[12] Other responses to corresponding programs include *Because Library Playdates Aren't Just for Kids* and *Because Homework Shouldn't Cause Headaches.*[13]

Another useful and thoughtfully written toolkit was developed by the Illinois Library Association entitled *Advocacy Toolkit: The Importance and Purpose of Library Advocacy*. This resource is a twelve-page treasure trove. Each section commences with questions or headings including "Why be a Library Advocate?" and "Who Should be a Library Advocate?"[14] Check out the resource here: https://www.ila.org/content/documents/ila-advocacy-toolkit-013112.pdf.

The New Hampshire Library Association provides a list of library advocacy links, which include NH Public Library Statistics, IMLS (Institute of Museum and Library) Surveys and Data, OCLC (formerly known as the Online Computer Library Center) From Awareness to Funding: Voter Perceptions and Support of Public Libraries in 2018 Report, Pew Research Center, and the Library Use Value (ROI) Calculator.[15] These are helpful resources to use in support of libraries, but the ROI calculator is an easy-to-provide, value-driven tool that shows in financial terms just how much money one saves while using library materials; simply input the number of materials used each month—such as adult, young adult, or children's titles checked out in a month, CDs checked out, newspapers read, meeting room use, programs attended, and more and you get an excellent bottom line of money saved. I just tested out the calculator,[16] and this month (with nine days left to go), I've saved $284. What better way to show patrons the value of the library! Be sure to check out the advocacy resources in your state, and if none exist, consider creating them.

These advocacy tools are so important for today's librarian—the shifting landscape of library services may not be on everyone's radar; there is still a population of people who believe libraries merely provide books. Mentioned at the beginning of this chapter, even though my dad was joking, I do wonder if people actually believe that all we do as library staff is read books! It's incumbent upon the librarian to help educate the public about library offerings and value as well as ensuring that children's services are adequately funded. Stand up on your soap box and advocate!

DIGITAL PREPAREDNESS FOR CHILDREN'S LIBRARIANS

Expect, welcome, and embrace change. This is the best advice for librarians and their relationship with technology. It's changing more quickly than we can keep up with, but we need to stay current with the most updated digital offerings for the sake of our young patrons. The authors Adele Fasick and Leslie Edmonds Holt refer to this relationship between librarians and technology as being in a state of perpetual beta. Doesn't that fit perfectly? "We can expect changes in the building we work in, the resources we offer, the way we deliver services, and the people we serve. Libraries are not monuments to the past but pathways to the future."[17] This is a great perspective to begin our discussion of technological competency in the library.

Libraries have really shifted in their information roles from being asked for an answer and providing it, to helping patrons locate vetted information for themselves. Adapting to the shifting roles is an art, so consider yourself more of a guide to information or an assistant to patrons in locating the information they need. To do this, have a fundamental understanding of the technologies being offered and being used by our young patrons and their caregivers; understand the digital collection and know how to locate information available online. This helps ensure that information is accessible and that you know how to find it.

One of the best technological skillsets I've found is from boltjobs.com in a June 2023 offering entitled "Top 10 Skills Every Librarian Needs to Succeed in Today's Digital World." They are:

1. Digital Literacy
2. Information Management
3. Technology Proficiency
4. Research Skills
5. Data Analysis
6. Communication Skills
7. Teaching and Instructional Skills
8. Adaptability
9. Critical Thinking
10. Customer Service Skills[18]

A rather broad scope of skills, to be sure, but a comprehensive list that will qualify you for today's librarianship; to learn more details, check this site: https://www.boltjobs.com/blog/skills-librarians-need-digital.

In addition to this list, the ALSC provides an abundance of information on the topic—from updated resources around digital offerings to Media Mentorship in Libraries Serving Youth to several helpful survey infographics, you can explore this site to sharpen your skills; head to https://www.ala.org/alsc/publications-resources/white-papers/mediamentorship.

If you're already in the profession and are working as a children's librarian, some of the practical applications of technology that you likely use every day include writing and distributing a newsletter utilizing a product like Constant

Contact, producing a monthly calendar of events, creating announcement flyers for programs—maybe using Canva, assisting young patrons with searching online, troubleshooting youth services computers, utilizing the library's ILS (integrated library system) at the circulation desk and to access their accounts to verify information, assisting young patrons with their devices (although they may sometimes be helping you!), enhancing program offerings—for example, by including a Minecraft club which uses a LAN (local area network)—using movie projection devices, and more. During the early months of the Covid-19 pandemic, many libraries offered online programs and book club discussions via Zoom or other virtual software. Some libraries have even kept their online programming as an option or have moved to hybrid offerings because they recognized that so many patrons were able to connect in this way. Understanding patron needs and the many uses of technology is key, and with an open mind, the librarian will come to realize there's no end to the ways that technology plays an important role in the offerings for their patrons.

In addition to knowing and understanding today's technology, the children's librarian must also have awareness of the impact of these technologies on children. In my Materials for Young Adults course, one of the weekly topics focuses on teens and their use of phones—we explore both the positive and negative impacts of this technology. Thinking about children and their brain development, a good question to examine is how screen time impacts a child's brain development. In an exploration piece by Rachel Nard, some of the questions around technology and children's programming in the library include "how much tech exposure is balanced, and how much is too much? What is the library's role in providing technological access to kids? What is our role in combating the digital divide in our communities and providing kids and families access to tech tools? How do we incorporate technology in ways which are intentional, balanced, engaging, interactive and developmentally appropriate for even our youngest library users?"[19] Responses to these questions helped form the basis for a Carnegie Library of Pittsburgh project to bring iPads into library programming with children.

Looking at some data on screen time for young children, the National University's website on the topic cites that the Mayo Clinic recommends limiting screen time for children between the ages of two and five to only one hour per day. Negative impacts of overuse of children and technology include obesity issues, social development impacts, and attention span problems.[20] Thinking about library offerings, it will be important to consider how and whether programming is planned around screen time.

As a child of the television age, I've had my share of screen time! I was a latch-key kid who came home to watch *Gilligan's Island* every day. I am not sure how that may have impacted me, but looking at today's young people, they contend with many more screens; ever-present phones travel with them to school and they have them at home and pretty much everywhere they go.

Being informed is so important for childhood development, and the librarian can be useful in educating caregivers around phone and screen safety; helping caregivers navigate the technology landscape by offering programs for them addressing technology and its impacts would be useful.

MANAGEMENT AND LEADERSHIP

There are natural managers and leaders, and there are some who need to learn the ropes of management and leadership. I fall squarely into the latter group. I came to the youth department as the head of youth services, having never been responsible for anyone but myself at work; I've made mistakes and learned a lot. I'm still navigating those waters all these years later and still falter. To be a good manager or leader is to embrace a dedication to learning, growing, adjusting, and embracing a lifelong learning approach—one of the first lessons I've learned. The second thing I've found immensely helpful is to lead with humility and honesty. Have you ever realized you made a mistake with staff? Maybe you were having a bad day, you may have been stressed, or maybe you didn't have the information you needed—whatever the reason, admit it to them, apologize, and show your willingness to learn to do better by mentioning your specific goals. Lying to cover up a mistake is never a good choice, but I've seen it happen with youth directors who have unfortunately lost the trust of their staff and have diminished their effective leadership. Avoid this pitfall! The precepts I try to embrace are my "four Cs": Compassion, Clarity, Connection, and a Commitment to Lifelong Learning.

I began my MLIS several years after I had already been in the position of head of youth services, so I seized the opportunity to learn more in a class that took a deep dive into supervisory and management skills. That helped me considerably, but it wasn't until I began working with people and putting those theories into practice, along with finding my own style, that I learned what an effective manager/leader looks like.

Before breaking down the four Cs, let's look at the difference between management and leadership; I'll start with definitions. This characterization of management is derived from G. Edward Evans and Stacey Greenwell's fourth edition of *Management Basics for Information Professionals*. It goes like this: "Management is the art of getting things done through people."[21] The authors go on to mention an additional option, noting that there is likely a myriad of other definitions out there: "Management is an activity essential to organized endeavors that perform certain functions to obtain the effective acquisition, allocation, and utilization of human efforts and physical resources for the purpose of accomplishing some goal."[22] Even Evans and Greenwell admit the first definition to be impersonal and simplistic; there is truly nothing in that definition that helps a manager do well. The second definition, while a bit bloated, encompasses a more well-rounded look into the meaning of the word.

It may be helpful to understand management through an anecdote: When a manager is asked what they do, there are often replies of attending to crises, solving issues that arise, or fielding complaints. Never, according to an older edition, this time authored by Evans and Patricia Ward, does a manager typically respond that they "direct, plan, control, delegate, budget, and hire and fire people."[23] These are, in fact, the tasks of the manager and are the building blocks of management.

Leadership is, according to Evans and Ward, "A collaborative activity generating the opportunity for all members of an organization to engage in the visioning and motivation of one another to meet the challenges of a continually changing operating environment."[24] This definition necessarily engages people and is a departure from the staid concept of management, but when a manager is also a leader, the excitement begins! Not all leaders in an organization may be managers, but managers must adopt leadership qualities—in my mind—to be effective. I have found that successful and often inclusive leadership creates a more conducive atmosphere in which managerial tasks may be more easily completed.

Some final words on management and leadership before moving on: between my spouse and me, we have experienced firsthand, over the course of our working lives, both great leaders and excellent managers as well as disorganized, sloppy, uncaring, and even toxic managers. We strive to learn from them and to carry out many of the qualities we have found to be the most successful, avoiding those that are unhelpful or harmful. Indeed.com, self-described as the number-one job site in the world, lists twenty qualities of good leaders—they are: hardworking, open-minded, empathetic, visionary, confident, honorable, ethical, positive, humble, communicative, decisive, courageous, able to delegate, accountable, resilient, passionate, disciplined, motivating, loyal, and consistent.[25] Whew! I think this is a lofty list of qualities, but it's a good list. I recommend writing these down in a prominent spot on your desk and reviewing them each morning as you prepare for the day. Seriously!

Now, I'll get to my four Cs, which share some elements of the Indeed.com list. I'll start with Compassion. Leading with an iron hand doesn't go very far. It creates negativity and resentment and shows a disregard for the human beings you're leading. Consider taking a compassionate approach. That old adage about walking in someone else's shoes can be useful here. Attempting to see the other person's perspective, caring about how they see what's happening, listening to the person, and mirroring back what you're hearing is not just good advice for managers and leaders, but it's also good for all relationships.

Clarity is next, but it might be simply called "communication." To effectively bring people on board with your management tasks, communicate clearly and directly what you're expecting (and hopefully this is something that you've already collaborated on with your staff), and how to achieve that task.

I can't emphasize enough the idea of Connection, our next "C." Bridging the managerial mindset to find ways to connect with colleagues and staff is to be human. By finding connection, you're necessarily working to understand them, to figure out ways to reach people and find common ground. I love this Australian College of Applied Professions discussion on the need for connection in the workplace: "People with good connections are happier, less stressed, more engaged at work and even physically healthier. In the workplace, these links help us learn, become engaged in what we're doing and feel loyal to our workplace."[26]

I've mentioned this already, but humility is required to be a good manager and leader. Knowing that there is so much we don't know but are willing to learn is priceless. So that brings us to the fourth "C": Commitment to Lifelong Learning. Reaching back to that library mission statement at the start of this chapter, this is another reminder that the librarian, but most especially the manager and leader, must embrace self-education. Also, a librarian who embraces learning will encourage colleagues to do the same. When things are not working well, find an effective and positive way to make changes, accept mistakes that were made, learn from them, and forge a new path moving forward. Sadly, though, if too much damage has occurred, the manager may have lost the trust and respect of their staff, and regaining that trust and respect is a hard-won battle.

There is no shortage of texts on management, particularly related to business; when I was in grad school, students were required to read Daniel Pink's *A Whole New Mind: Why Right-Brainers Will Rule the Future*. It's a fascinating text that really resonated with me. Reading about the hemispheres of the brain and his description of the six senses was revelatory; I especially enjoyed the anecdotes Pink included to illustrate his points. You might want to check out this book as well as others he's written.

I work hard to improve my management and leadership skills by exploring the latest offerings, and the most recent book I've been reading is *Best Team Ever!: The Surprising Science of High Performing Teams* by David Burkus. Focusing on a triangular approach to create a high-functioning team, the three areas are: have common understanding, psychological safety, and prosocial purpose.[27] Several concepts mirror information already mentioned in this section, but this is a welcome reminder that takes the concepts and organizes them in a unique way. I'm finding Burkus's perspective helpful.

But wait—there's more! Reading several of the myriad titles available on leadership and management can be helpful in finding your own path, and it is incumbent upon you to take in all manner of management and leadership methods—explore widely! Once you've hopefully found something that resonates with you, make it your own, find your voice and your own style, and forge your unique path to management and leadership excellence.

BUDGETS AND FUNDING

While this is not among my favorite topics, it's an important one to consider in the administration of children's services. Before offering various perspectives, note that libraries, depending on size, location, and extent of their support, will vary widely in their financial resources. My own experience has been kind of interesting. While I was always provided with a firm collection development budget with monthly updates on amounts spent and remaining for the year, I never actually had a clearly defined programming budget; much of the reason for this is that children's programming was funded by several entities. The Friends of the Library funded the summer reading program, successful grant applications from various charitable donations funded unique programs, and then there was the actual programming budget shared with adult services programming. If I wanted to offer a program, I simply checked in with the director, who let me know whether this would work as well as determining the funding source. I realize that most libraries work within a tight budget framework; in that case, your budget is clear.

Each year, the library director has the responsibility of presenting the upcoming year's budget to the municipality, which will hopefully be supported and adopted by governing boards. In doing so, often the director will review the past year's expenses and revenues to help justify the next year's budget, which would likely outline a clear path for future financial requisitions and would include various funding sources and methods of overseeing the expenditures including recordkeeping. The person responsible for the youth department would likely provide the library director with similar information, specific to the youth department and within the parameters set by the director. Still, the annual ritual of budgeting may not necessarily include all library staff who are tasked with program planning. As in my experience, funding sources may be coming from outside the adopted budget, such as the Friends group, and without specific funding numbers—as in my case—one may present program expenditure requests for approval throughout the year. Regardless of funding sources, a good plan for the budget cycle is needed, and working with the library director or the head of youth services to better understand funding mechanisms and the budgeting process is always good practice.

Once again, advocacy plays a vital role as the youth department staff may be required to provide reasoning for requested funds. In this case, it's critical that librarians are prepared to defend how and why a program may be included in the library's offerings. It's not enough to simply go on the assumption that funding will be available because kids like certain books or whatever the focus of a program may be—there needs to be an understanding of how the funding will further the patrons' enlightenment; in short, how does each program meet the stated goals of the mission statement? Be prepared to create your programming with the end in mind—this isn't the first time I've mentioned this! Here, you're literally providing sound reasons why a program should take place. This becomes even more important in the rare library, which often focuses on adult services and not as much on children's services. Be clear, vocal, concise, and utilize all aspects of advocacy, especially performance measures, that, coupled with your knowledge of children's developmental needs and how the library meets those needs, will help you to secure needed funding. Many libraries are struggling with funding, so creating multiple revenue sources, measuring any volunteer time or donations in reporting resources, creating partnerships with local businesses, and reporting on the success of programming through the numbers of participants will enhance your budget and showcase your willingness to think outside the budget box.

So, how do you create that sound budget? Evans and Ward offer the following four steps, and I encourage you to examine them a bit more deeply, but these steps are clear within themselves. They are:

1. Determine ongoing and desirable programs and establish priorities.
2. Estimate the plans for each unit in monetary terms.
3. Combine all estimates into a well-balanced program. This will require investigation of each plan's financial feasibility and a comparison of the program with institutional goals.
4. Compare, for a given time, the estimates derived from Step 3 with the actual results, making corrections for any significant differences. (Use the budget as a standard for appraising the performance of the budget manager.)[28]

When creating these budgets, Evans and Ward mention four types of budgets: a materials budget, a labor budget, a distribution/expense budget, and an administrative budget.[29] Think of the materials budget as the physical supplies required for operating the library. The labor budget is the amount spent on employee work hours. "The distribution/expense budget considers the estimated costs of services and record keeping. Distribution expenses are generally subdivided in terms of departmental responsibility; for example, public services and branch operations."[30] Lastly, the administrative expense budget are those funds that are spent in actual managerial tasks like traveling expenses, as an example.[31]

Should you find yourself in the position of budget creation, defense, and implementation, you'll have a learning curve, to be sure—from zero-based budgets to audits, you'll need to explore all aspects of budget creation and implementation carefully. A good place to start is an outline of the budget creation process found in the Maine Library Trustee Handbook; you can find that document at https://www.maine.gov/msl/libs/admin/documents/Chapter14_OCR.pdf.[32] This includes a foundational look at budget creation that includes The Budget Development Process, Sources of Funding, Desirable Budget Characteristics, Types of Budgets, and Sources of Additional Information.[33] Along with this document, don't miss Evans and Ward's *Management Basics for Information Professionals*.

Important additional sources of funding include grants and gifts or donations. While this and other budgetary concerns may fall outside your job description, awareness of grant opportunities is an option to explore beyond the set budgetary funds. As part of my graduate work, I included a course on grant writing—what a boon to the library! I was able to write, implement, and report on a grant that benefited several population groups in the community.

Grants are often specific to a one-time project, and the writing of grants is a learned process; there are many moving parts, and it takes finesse and a clear vision to secure funding as you're competing with others for those same funds, but don't despair! Grant-writing advice is available and easily found online, there are grant-writing classes, and you may even seek out a grant-writing mentor.

Sources of grant funding for libraries can be found online as well. Consider the Institute of Museum and Library Services (IMLS) grant opportunities. This federal program's website is a treasure trove of information that includes information on how to apply for a grant, how to manage grants, a list of grants available to you, as well as a listing of grants and monies that have been awarded.[34]

EBSCO Connect (https://connect.ebsco.com/s/article/Grants-Funding-Sources-for-Libraries?language=en_US) includes a Grant and Funding Sources for Library section that provides extensive information about available grants as well as tips on how to write them.[35]

These are two outstanding sources for grants, but don't be limited by them! Even a rudimentary search will yield unique grant opportunities that may be specific to the project you have in mind. As with children's programming, when I recommended searching online for ideas, I do the same here—search far and wide by adjusting your search terms, and you'll find no end to the opportunities available for libraries and children's services.

You may have a regular source of funding in your library that is derived from a charitable donation; at my library, we're lucky to have consistent donations that directly impact professional development from a #1 *New York Times* bestselling author who lives in town. Due to this generosity, professional development is fully funded, ensuring an even more robust programming budget. Perhaps there is an opportunity for your library in this area as well.

Friends of the Library groups may also offer funding beyond the budgetary cycle funds. They may support the youth department in specific ways—like funding a summer reading program, or they may be receptive to helping fund specific programs. In this case, you'll once again be required to make a case for your request.

Depending on your library's policies, you might opt to seek donations of materials by posting a wish list on your website, or you may include a plea in the library's newsletter. Even a sign announcing your wish list at the circulation desk might help to get the needed items.

I'd like to end this section with an idea mentioned by Evans and Ward, and that is that those who manage budgets and are tasked with securing funding may sometimes be unsuccessful. However, they state that it may be due not to your shortcomings but to economic situations, and "by preparing solid requests, having a track record of careful and thoughtful stewardship of funds granted, providing high-quality service to the user community, and having realistic but forward looking plans you will, more often than not, secure the maximum possible funding."[36] I like that idea of stewardship and will end on that note.

OUTREACH AND MARKETING

One of my favorite stories of outreach is a collaboration that I had the opportunity to form with a local organization called Seacoast Outright; I connected with the group to share LGBTQ book talks and eventually became a volunteer facilitator. All in all, it was a rewarding experience. Outreach and partnerships with local organizations strengthen the library in the community and allow for resource sharing—among other benefits. Related, the concept of marketing for the library is unique; while the library doesn't technically have anything to market as far as retail items, it does need to be concerned with branding and could use some pointers from the business sector on how to promote itself. In this section, I'll examine these two important areas—outreach and marketing—that connect libraries with their communities.

As has been the case in other areas of this book, the first place to begin when considering outreach is to develop an awareness of existing opportunities for youth in the community; an example in Rye, New Hampshire, is the presence of a skate park for youth; the library had a program in which kids read ten books and got free admission to the park—they loved this! Awareness of existing opportunities also opens the door to develop connections with businesses and agencies, including neighboring community libraries; this enables a resource-sharing opportunity, according to Susan Higgins in *Youth Services and Public Libraries*.[37] Remember to include outreach that will benefit the diverse population—so get creative with how you link to other entities to advance the library's mission.

Once an assessment is complete around community offerings, think about areas that may provide a collaboration. You might be surprised to discover that some unlikely businesses would form a unique partnership. In a beach town, try reaching out to the surf shop. Consider the many crafts that you do or could do in your makerspaces and connect to businesses like bead shops, embroidery shops, and stores such as Joann Fabrics or Michaels—in what ways can the library promote the business while enhancing the library's program offerings?

You might consider approaching a bead store, as an example, and set up a system in which librarians can learn to weave and make various bracelets and other beaded items at the cost of only materials, and then can teach those crafts to older elementary-aged patrons all while letting patrons know they can purchase more materials from the store at a discounted price; in this scenario, everyone wins! This example is rooted in a long partnership I created with a local bead store, and truly, patrons benefitted. I had the pleasure of learning weaving patterns for free, and the store saw an increase in customers who received a library discount when making purchases. I loved this collaboration.

Several benefits of outreach should convince you that outreach is beneficial in the public library. One unique benefit of outreach involves connecting with diverse members of the community who may otherwise not frequent the library, thereby increasing library patronage and community engagement. Building awareness around library offerings necessarily increases community members' access to information; many people may simply not be aware of the library's services. Focusing on outreach efforts also increases and promotes literacy—by reaching out to various demographics like children and non-native speakers, programming can be tailored specifically to their needs. Important partners in youth departments are schools; by collaborating with teachers, school media specialists, and the school administration, the library's resources are made available and thereby support education. Finally, the library might act as a cultural center for diverse groups of people and utilizing outreach can develop partnerships by fostering dialogue and tolerance in the community.

I like the possibilities offered by Penny Peck in her book *Crash Course in Children's Services*; the list may include entities that you may not have considered: farmer's markets, the local mall, businesses for prize donations, local access cable TV and local newspapers, pediatricians, museums (especially those that are children-oriented), and the YMCA and Boys and Girls Clubs.[38] I can speak to the farmer's market option as I had the pleasure of going to the farmer's market across the street from the library; each week I'd bring over a small chair, some books, and a blanket, and offered kids a storytime while their caregivers were shopping. This was so much fun and brought new patrons to the library who hadn't considered visiting.

Outreach is all about connections, but in the process of forming these connections, there is, at least in part, the additional benefit of helping market the library. Library marketing: It sounds kind of funny, right? I think of marketing as belonging exclusively to retail and other business offerings, and since we don't serve customers, we serve patrons, this seems to make some sense—but consider whether there really is a difference. The library can directly impact its relevance by touting its wares, so to speak. There are many benefits to marketing in libraries, and the first consideration is the furthering of its mission. If the goal, as seen with the Rye Public Library, is to encourage lifelong learning, how can that happen if people don't know what the library does? I've mentioned it before, but many people still have a somewhat stuffy view of shushing librarians and dusty books in quiet, dimly lit stacks. If only they were at the library after school!

Marketing increases awareness of libraries and the wide range of services they have to offer. The library where I work, as well as those I've frequented, are often considered community centers; increasing awareness of the library's presence as a community hub can lead to increased patronage. Marketing can help community members see the array of digital resources available—databases, language-learning platforms, and even college-like courses. By including some of this in marketing strategies, these resources will be used and appreciated. A strong marketing campaign that fully represents all the resources and programming available will help the library show its relevance in this digital age. Additionally, effective marketing can reach local government, library stakeholders, and resident voters who can potentially determine whether to fund and support the library in the future. Finally, and this meets the mission of the library, marketing can simply promote and increase literacy. Overall, the library can be a community hub, but in order to achieve this, the library needs to use shameless self-promotion and market itself by showcasing all it has to offer.

In *5 Marketing Strategies to Promote Your Library*, the New Jersey State Library offers these options to promote the library: social media marketing, email marketing, search engine optimization, video marketing, and event marketing.[39] I have to say, a library in the town adjacent to where I work has a small A-frame style messaging board that is used to consistently market programs. This is a great tool for busy families that don't have the time to visit social media or websites to keep up with the latest events. The A-frame is the perfect draw for the last-minute type of shopper, or, in this case, a patron who opts to join an event on the spur of the moment.

Libraries often don't have the funding to hire a dedicated staff member to exclusively do outreach and marketing; instead, it's usually the responsibility of the program lead or, in a larger library, junior staff to perform these duties. As staffing has become somewhat of an issue over the past few years, it's likely that for a smaller library, everyone will need to be well-versed in outreach and marketing techniques. Again, regarding lifelong learning for the librarian, it's a good idea to read widely on ways to effectively achieve outreach and marketing goals, especially as they relate to broadening library services, gaining community support, and supporting the library's mission and overarching goals.

PROFESSIONAL DEVELOPMENT

Congrats! You've landed the perfect job as a children's librarian. Now you can settle in and rest on your laurels—what you've learned in library school is enough, right? It's sad to report that some folks do enter the workforce and simply go with the flow, but the dynamic children's librarian knows the importance of being "in the know" on the latest technologies, the latest publishing trends, and what programs kids are interested in attending. Seeking out this information is great, but more formal professional development will not only advance your career but will also energize and excite you and will obviously transfer that knowledge and enthusiasm to your young patrons.

I have had incredible experiences attending both local and national conferences, including ALA's annual conference, completing graduate school, taking part in webinars, and meeting with local librarians to chat about children's services. I've benefited from all these opportunities, but I have to say, meeting with other librarians in the local area has been one of the most rewarding through bouncing ideas off one another, discussing the nuances of patron interests at different libraries, and, most of all, getting very cool and exciting programming ideas; fellow librarians have been an incredible resource. One means to this end was volunteering on various award committees, which gave me another opportunity to meet with other librarians. In times when I was feeling stagnant, getting to those meetings, and absorbing the energy of other librarians proved worth the time and then some! Likewise, I shared my own exciting successes with others who might have found themselves stuck and needing a boost. Don't miss the chance to engage with librarians near you.

I've also very much enjoyed attending conferences where not only do you get a measure of the enthusiasm of shared librarian experiences, but you also benefit from the vast knowledge of presenters who have likely spent time educating themselves in the most current practices and topics. A notable moment in my life as a children's librarian attending conferences was when I had the chance to meet Dr. Betsey Diamant-Cohen, the founder of Mother Goose on the Loose (MGOL). Goodness. I could hardly speak for the rockstar status she held for me. I had been doing MGOL programming and constantly sought to improve and perfect my skills with that baby storytime, so seeing her perform the various elements of storytime in person was nothing short of miraculous! I went back to my library and immediately used my newly acquired skills to wonderful effect. I have never underestimated the power of professional development, and that's merely one small example of the many benefits I've derived from continued learning.

As I've done in previous sections, I'll begin with a working definition of professional development. According to *Professional Development Harvard Division of Continuing Education*, "Professional development is gaining new skills through continuing education and career training after entering the workforce. It can include taking classes or workshops, attending professional or industry conferences, or earning a certificate to expand your knowledge in your chosen field."[40] The most obvious benefit of professional development is how it leads to better service for your patrons, but don't underestimate the benefits of both increasing the possibility of promotions within the library as well as enhancing your resumé.

Really, the learning never ends in the position of a children's librarian as the landscape of service to patrons is constantly shifting—some of the reasons to remain current include providing STEM and STEAM programming, evaluating literary and educational trends, including makerspaces in the library, or possibly creating a library of things. There are many opportunities for growth and development. It's likely that by the time this text is published, new and exciting possibilities are in the works for library patrons, so here are some areas to further your knowledge.

Among the library professional development options, Michael Sullivan outlines the following in *Fundamentals of Children's Services*:

- Conferences and Classes
- Professional Reading
- Committee and Organization Work
- Mentoring
- Writing, Speaking, and Teaching[41]

I've touched on conferences and classes, but keeping up with the profession involves professional reading. New books are a good resource; I often visit the American Library Association store to see the latest. Journals like *School Library Journal, American Libraries Magazine*, and *The Horn Book* offer not only collection development opportunities but also include the latest in library trends and reviews of professional titles. Exploring EBSCO and seeking out articles online again offers some of the most current reading for the librarian. Check publishing websites, and ensure you broaden that exploration to independent publishers that offer titles not often found in library journals.

I started my library career by immediately diving into The Flume: New Hampshire Teen Reader's Choice Award. I discovered this award committee just at the end of my time as a middle school teacher and could not wait to jump in when I landed my youth services librarian position. I loved the work—which was so joyful. I mean, what's not to love about chatting with other librarians about books? Working on this committee, I forged friendships that have lasted years, learned so much more about teen literature, and gained confidence in collection development. Similarly, when I participated as a committee member on the Great Stone Face Book Award for children in grades four to six, I added to my competency in teen collection development to juvenile-aged literature in the same way.

Sullivan mentions mentoring on the list. I had the unique opportunity to be both mentored and act as a mentor to other librarians. When I started my career in libraries, I was petrified to do storytime. I had no experience working with children of this age aside from caring for my baby sister when I was ten. How do you engage babies? I felt confident working with middle-school-aged students, but babies? I reached out to libraries in the area and attended several storytimes, and a baby lapsit program leader inspired me to the point that, to this day, many years later, I remember the details of her expertise that I employed at storytime. It's also been wonderful offering my knowledge base to those new librarians who in turn needed my assistance.

Finally, writing, speaking, and teaching are on Sullivan's list. I can tell you, to teach is to learn. I was never so great at grammar as when I had to teach it to students. Teaching requires a depth of knowledge that you don't have when you merely set out to learn something. It requires that you think differently from the perspective of those who don't know about the topic so that you get to the crux of the information to convey it to others in a variety of ways to accommodate different learning styles. Writing is similar, and many librarians write book reviews, articles, and even books on topics related to children's librarianship. As you continue the path of your own career, consider how you might impart your own knowledge and experiences to your fellow colleagues. In what way can you add to the breadth of information in your profession? Think about writing in some way. And similarly, have you considered speaking at a local or national conference on your areas of expertise or interest? Once again, this requires that you learn and understand in a way that others can digest and understand; you necessarily become something of an expert in the area about which you're presenting.

Sullivan's five bulleted items mentioned earlier are important areas to explore, and to those, I'd like to add examining blogs! Goodness, I've benefited so much from "Don't Shush Me" (more focused on teens) as well as "jbrary"—a blog focused specifically on storytimes and more generally on services to children. Visit their site and prepare to be amazed! While you're there, you can link to, at last count, 172 other youth services sites and blogs under the blogroll tab. So much to explore!

Another invaluable source for professional development is adding yourself to library listservs. There's nothing more illuminating than being on a listserv that addresses topics pertinent to your work. A programming listserv for the specific age groups you work with will delight you. Belonging to various listservs may also provide opportunities for further professional development. As an example, I answered a listserv call for potential topics for a teen library series and landed a book deal on serving LGBTQ teens in the library. So cool!

Finally, a well-rounded children's librarian will explore beyond the library world by keeping current in the fields of education, child welfare, and child psychology. Other professions often shed light on library services in unexpected and useful ways. As an example, my spouse, a regional land-use planner, has involved librarians in several of her planning programs that emphasize age-friendly communities and even featured local librarians and programs that supported younger and older patrons coming together to learn from one another.

I've managed to cast a wide net in so many areas of librarianship, and I encourage you to do the same for library professional development.

This chapter has provided a structure for administration and professional development in youth services. A good youth library head or director will employ some of these methodologies, but a great one will find a way to create their own pathway, will consider all that is offered here, and inspire their staff to engage fully in their work with children.

REVIEW QUESTIONS

1. Discuss the goals and benefits of lifelong learning through the lens of both patrons and librarians.
2. Compare/contrast the five laws of librarianship according to Ranganathan (search for these online) and compare those to Virginia Walter's laws specific to youth librarianship.
3. According to Karis Loop, what three areas are stated as desired outcomes or competencies for each age group she mentions? Also, what is meant by "inching up the ramp" in Loop's work?
4. Are advocacy and marketing related? Outline similarities and differences you may determine.
5. List the top ten skills needed for youth librarian digital preparedness; dig more deeply to include descriptions of each of the ten areas. Do these still resonate with the times? What other preparedness might be included?
6. Outline the differences between management and leadership. Reflect on an employer you've worked with and determine what qualities they possess. Are they leaders? Managers? Both?
7. Research and report on at least three grants that you would consider landing for your library. Describe the desired outcomes, the requirements to apply, and reporting that may be required after the grant has been awarded.
8. Research and report on an upcoming conference of interest to you and include the specific sessions you'd plan to attend; how will these sessions improve your work in the library? If you're not employed by a library, conduct the research and report on how you think the sessions would be helpful.
9. Select any area in this chapter and conduct research to obtain current professional articles and report on those articles in a short essay.

NOTES

1. Rye Public Library Board of Trustees, "Library Mission and Vision Statements," accessed October 22, 2023, https://ryepubliclibrary.org/library-mission-statements/.
2. Virginia A. Walter, *Children & Libraries: Getting It Right* (Chicago: ALA Editions, 2001), 123.
3. Karis Loop, *Seamless Youth Services for Every Age and Stage* (Chicago: ALA Editions, 2019), vii.
4. Ibid, xii.
5. Ibid, xiii.

6. Association for Library Service to Children, "Competencies for Librarians Serving Children in Libraries," accessed October 22, 2023, https://www.ala.org/alsc/edcareeers/alsccorecomps.
7. Alliance for Justice, "What is Advocacy?: Definitions and Examples," accessed October 22, 2023, https://mffh.org/wp-content/uploads/2016/04/AFJ_what-is-advocacy.pdf.
8. Lisa Houde, in Kay Ann Cassell, *Public Libraries and Their Communities* (Lanham, MD: Rowman & Littlefield, 2021), 141.
9. Melissa Gross, Cindy Mediavilla, and Virgina A. Walter, *5 Steps of Outcome-Based Planning for Youth Services* (Chicago: ALA Editions, 2022).
10. Cecilia Freda, "Promoting Your Library Program: Getting the Message Out." *Knowledge Quest* 36, no. 1 (2007): 48+. Gale Academic OneFile (accessed February 7, 2024). https://link.gale.com/apps/doc/A172383305/AONE?u=anon-4a7310f&sid=googleScholar&xid=49fd1c84.
11. Lesley S. J. Farmer, *Impactful Community-Based Literacy Projects* (Chicago: ALA Editions, 2021), 115.
12. Erica Ruscio, "Everyday Advocacy: Doing What You Do," accessed October 22, 2023, https://journals.ala.org/index.php/cal/article/view/7378/10147.
13. Association for Library Service to Children, "Championing Children's Services Toolkit," accessed October 22, 2023, https://www.ala.org/alsc/sites/ala.org.alsc/files/content/initiatives/everydayadvocacy/ALSC-Championing-Childrens-Services-Toolkit.pdf.
14. Illinois Library Association, "Advocacy Toolkit: The Importance and Purpose of Library Advocacy," accessed October 22, 2023, https://www.ila.org/content/documents/ila-advocacy-toolkit-013112.pdf.
15. New Hampshire Library Association, "Advocacy Resources," accessed October 22, 2023, https://nhlibrarians.org/Pages/Index/225187/advocacy-legislative-resources.
16. Maine State Library, "Library Use Value Calculator: What is Your Library Worth to You?," accessed October 22, 2023, https://www.maine.gov/msl/services/calculator.htm.
17. Adele M. Fasick and Leslie Edmonds Holt, *Managing Children's Services in Libraries, 4th Ed.* (Santa Barbara, CA: Libraries Unlimited, 2013), 206.
18. Boltjobs.com, "The Top 10 Skills Needed by Librarians in the Digital Age," accessed January 24, 2024, https://www.boltjobs.com/blog/skills-librarians-need-digital.
19. Rachel Nard, "All Hands on Tech: Exploring Technology in Kids Library Programming," accessed October 27, 2023, https://www.carnegielibrary.org/all-hands-on-tech-exploring-technology-in-kids-library-programming/.
20. National University, "The Negative Effects of Technology on Children," accessed October 27, 2023, https://www.nu.edu/blog/negative-effects-of-technology-on-children-what-can-you-do/.
21. G. Edward Evans and Stacey Greenwell, *Management Basics for Information Professionals, 4th Ed.* (Chicago: ALA Neal-Schuman, 2020), 5.
22. Ibid., 5-6.
23. G. Edward Evans and Patricia Layzell Ward, *Management Basics for Information Professionals, 2nd Ed.* (New York: Neal-Schuman Publishers, Inc., 2007), 8.
24. Ibid., 330.

25. Indeed for Employers, "Taking the Lead: A Leadership Qualities List for Effective Team Management," accessed October 24, 2023, https://www.indeed.com/hire/c/info/leadership-qualities-list.
26. Australian College of Applied Professions, "Connection in the Workplace," accessed October 23, 2023, https://www.acap.edu.au/newsletters/connection-in-the-workplace/.
27. David Burkus, *Best Team Ever!: The Surprising Science of High-Performing Teams* (Twinbolt, 2023), 2.
28. Evans and Ward, *Management Basics for Information Professionals, 2nd Ed.*, 408.
29. Ibid., 420.
30. Ibid., 420.
31. Ibid., 420.
32. Maine Library Trustee Handbook, "Developing the Library Budget," accessed October 26, 2023, https://www.maine.gov/msl/libs/admin/documents/Chapter14_OCR.pdf.
33. Ibid.
34. Institute of Museum and Library Services, "Grants," accessed October 26, 2023, https://www.imls.gov/grants.
35. Ebsco Connect, "Grants & Funding Sources for Libraries," accessed October 26, 2023, https://connect.ebsco.com/s/article/Grants-Funding-Sources-for-Libraries?language=en_US.
36. Evans and Ward, *Management Basics for Information Professionals, 2nd Ed.*, 406.
37. Susan E. Higgins, *Youth Services and Public Libraries* (Oxford: Chandos Publishing, 2007), 118.
38. Penny Peck, *Crash Course in Children's Services, 2nd Ed.* (Santa Barbara, CA: Libraries Unlimited, 2014), 94.
39. New Jersey State Library, "5 Marketing Strategies to Promote Your Library," accessed October 27, 2023, https://www.njstatelib.org/5-marketing-strategies-to-promote-your-library/.
40. Professional Development Harvard Division of Continuing Education, "Why is Professional Development Important?," accessed October 27, 2023, https://professional.dce.harvard.edu/blog/why-is-professional-development-important/.
41. Michael Sullivan, *Children's Services, 2nd Ed.* (Chicago: ALA Editions, 2013), 299.

9

Looking Ahead

WHAT'S NEXT IN LIBRARY SERVICES FOR CHILDREN

dNo one can predict the future with any certainty, but libraries can examine five areas for guidance: current demographic statistics/demographic shifts and projections, technological developments, educational trends, inclusive and diverse materials collections, and actual building space needs. Looking at these areas will help guide strategic planning and prepare for future generations of library patrons beyond the typical five-year strategic plan.

Reflecting on the history of libraries, the nation has experienced a significant shift from libraries as "just a place to get books" to becoming a community center around which activities are planned. The library has become a place to connect people to information, connect librarians and their patrons, and, more importantly, connect to the community and to one another. I'll discuss this further in this chapter, but beyond the benefits that technology offers, people deeply desire connection with other people—in person and not just through social media.

In *Library NEXT: 7 Action Steps for Reinvention*, Catherine Murray-Rust encourages libraries to reinvent themselves by utilizing seven action steps that expand beyond the walls of the library, but before doing that, she admonishes to look inward—to look at both the community and at yourself.[1] I love this concept. In fact, Murray-Rust's book is an excellent resource for the library seeking to prepare for the future in strategic planning or simply to consider what may be the best ways to serve the community beyond today's offerings. I won't discuss all seven steps, but I'm especially drawn to the second action step: Be Curious About the Future—here, a key takeaway is to think about the future not necessarily as a continuation of the present but to try to imagine different futures utilizing stories.[2] In other words, be curious and creative in thinking about how to best serve library users in the future. In this chapter, I'll take a quick peek into what the future of libraries may look like and how librarians may prepare for radical changes in these five areas; I'll view the five areas both for libraries generally and, more specifically, on potential impacts for youth.

LIBRARIES SERVE PEOPLE: WHO ARE THE PEOPLE IN YOUR NEIGHBORHOOD?

At its foundation—stripping away the energy spent on creating various services—the library is about serving people, and the future of libraries is certainly also about people. The past and present have been and are also about people, though, but looking to the future of libraries requires thoughtful examinations in two areas: first, as has often been mentioned in this book, a wholehearted understanding of the community's people is needed through an examination of age profiles as well as diversity information to know the people you're serving, and second, to determine the needs of the people in your community based on the statistical information gathered.

KNOWING YOUR COMMUNITY DEMOGRAPHICS, TODAY AND TOMORROW

Conduct a Google search on population trends for your region and your state, and you may be surprised to learn how demographics are shifting. Although there are a few states that are seeing a rise in younger age cohorts, for the most part, the nation is aging as the baby boomers advance in years and younger adults are having fewer children. This has resulted in a strained workforce, smaller households, and a decline in school enrollment. How will these changes in demographics impact library services? Library programs must shift toward more all-inclusive programs that might attract people of all ages if they don't already. Along those lines, programs may attract multigenerational patrons, such as teens aiding older adults with their IT devices, storytimes with grandparents, and family storytimes. Aside from age trends, librarians may want to learn their community's demographic trends regarding race and ethnicity.

COLLECTIONS: DIVERSE AND INCLUSIVE

This time, when you search for demographic trends on Google, consider the trends that address race and ethnicity. Again, you may be surprised to learn that percentages of non-white races and diverse ethnicities are growing in many communities across the nation. If, indeed, your library's policy states that the collection must reflect its diverse population (and it should), then you want to understand what races and ethnicities make up your community. This will allow you to include more diverse titles on the shelves, which will, in turn, affirm to children and their families that the library is really prepared to serve people of varied origins and that their community library is embracing everyone, including them. Additionally, it provides all readers with possible new cultures and perspectives to discover, expanding their understanding and appreciation of people other than their own, and expanding their worldview.

Providing diverse titles can help encourage critical thinking, support education and learning, and help build empathy and understanding. Finally, acknowledging various and unique races and cultures provides new opportunities for the library to discover and build new relationships, programs, and the collection.

Ultimately, exploring shifting population dynamics will ensure a future that accurately serves the library's patrons.

Next is the need to understand the educational and entertainment needs of diverse populations and how they want to be connected; additionally, determine how that educational, entertainment, and connection will best serve the population—in other words, what is the delivery mechanism that best serves patrons today and well into the future?

Of course, when we think about the needs of patrons and look back over the history of how libraries have served patrons, it's clear that a discussion about technology is important. Before getting to that section, though, what I'm starting to understand is that more than technology, and especially after the pandemic, people are looking to engage with other people. Technology is great, but many patrons at the circulation desk are commenting to me that they just need to get out and engage with others. We've seen an increase in attendance for our adult book club and other programs, the youth department is burgeoning and expanding services to meet the needs of more children coming to the library after school, and the door count has risen significantly from pre-pandemic numbers. While technology is a factor and will be an important consideration for future library services, Barbra Streisand was spot on when she sang that "people who need people are the luckiest people in the world."

I had the unique opportunity as a graduate student to work with Dr. Michael Stephens, a professor at San José State University, and when he published his book *Whole-Hearted Librarianship: Finding Hope, Inspiration, and Balance*, I was thrilled; I couldn't wait to get my hands on a copy. It did not disappoint. Packed with sensitive and moving moments reflecting on library school, library service, and library students, the book inspires and informs. One particular takeaway that resonated with me was this thought about librarians: "We are the heart of our communities, and that only works because of what the people who run the libraries give of themselves. They do it knowing that there will be hard days and disappointment, budget fights, and individuals whom they may not be able to reach. The best librarians make that emotional investment because they believe in the institution and the communities they serve."[3] Isn't this just wonderful? And it really speaks to the need for connection.

Before moving on to community engagement and collaborations, a final look at connections to people is in order. As reported by *Medium*, "Social connection is an essential aspect of a healthy lifestyle and has even been reported to strengthen the immune system, help disease recovery times, and increase lifespan."[4] Did you know that? It's true! By providing programs and other library events, and even having the smallest positive interactions with a patron, the library is literally helping improve the health of its patrons. When thinking about how much work a program may be, consider the impact your work has, not just the immediate outcome of the craft, movie, or speaker presentation, but also on the well-being of the people in attendance. How gratifying!

I know several older patrons at the library who have lost their life partners and come to the library to pick up a book; in many instances, the interaction they have with the librarian may be the only in-person human connection they've had that day. I also think deeply about how social media and all this helpful technology might be impacting youth—they have a steady and high volume of information coming at them all the time—is it any wonder they're experiencing anxiety, depression, and feeling lonely? They're overwhelmed! Connecting to the librarian in short but meaningful conversations may just be the connection they need that day. It's true that you never know what's on the minds of those coming through the library doors; making space for people, being compassionate, and employing expert listening skills can be a game changer.

COMMUNITY ENGAGEMENT AND COLLABORATIONS

I see a future in which libraries are even more engaged with community stakeholders and employ deeper collaborations with schools and recreation and other community departments, local businesses, community volunteer boards, and other organizations. Why? It makes sense to fully utilize resources—both financial resources and in sharing personnel expertise—to create more impactful community service through enhanced quality of services as well as the reach of library offerings; this is a win-win-win scenario!

In addition to the benefits listed here, youth receive holistic and well-rounded support when community groups participate in education; libraries may offer supplemental resources, and community partners may offer extracurricular connections to the school curriculum, which permits schools to focus on more formal educational processes. This necessarily creates a truly comprehensive learning environment that addresses individualized learning needs.

Finally, and I've mentioned this before to some extent, when the entire community invests in a child's education, the success of instilling lifelong learning is increased dramatically; this collaboration fosters curiosity and intellectual exploration.

To summarize this section, I'd have to say that making connections—true, deeply felt emotional connections—to library patrons in addition to serving their informational needs is paramount. Harkening back to Stephens's 2019 book, he concurs that, despite the technological developments, "I've witnessed a conscious shift back to our spaces, our libraries, and how we welcome our users."[5] Based on my own observations, I could not agree more.

TECHNOLOGY: DIGITAL INTEGRATION AND VIRTUAL SERVICES... AND BEYOND

It goes without saying, but I'll say it anyway—technology is advancing at a breakneck speed, and libraries must not only keep up with that technology, but they must also excel in the library's technological offerings. Up until now, libraries have met the challenge of providing users with what they need and how they'd like to use it. I'm thinking of Hoopla, Libby, and other online resources readily available on a library's website. I currently get at least five calls per month from patrons who have questions about Hoopla. There's no doubt about it; patrons are consuming library materials differently, and libraries are meeting those needs. The key is, once again, to actively search out library trends in technology and determine whether they will offer the community something that will be helpful—not all technology is good technology; as with other materials, it's incumbent upon the librarian to understand the community and acquire those technologies that will truly serve the patrons' needs.

Among the considerations around technology is how the pandemic unearthed gaps in technology access for underserved populations; libraries need to look carefully at how they might help fill these gaps by providing better online access.

I'm mentioning artificial intelligence (AI) here, but the benefits and troublesome aspects of this rapidly evolving technology are far outside the scope of this chapter. Still, it's important to consider how the library may employ AI to better serve patrons. Charla Viera outlines five areas in which AI impacts libraries: "AI can improve information organization, accessibility, user services, and library analytics. It also emphasizes the importance of AI literacy for both librarians and patrons in today's society."[6] Careful considerations should be made around the efficacy of AI, and understanding the potential issues with AI should also be explored.

EDUCATIONAL TRENDS: STEM, STEAM

Looking to education can help inform how the library shapes its programming. Outlined here are education trends to consider, as referenced in Eric Debétaz's article "Top Education Trends to Watch For in 2024." They include:

1. Tech Trends in Teaching and Learning: Gamification, Blockchain, and AI and More
2. Soft Skills Training: Entrepreneurship, Public Speaking, and Leadership Skills

Looking Ahead

3. Decreasing Attention Spans: The Nano Learning Trend
4. Facilitating Learning vs. Teaching
5. Lifelong Learning Trend[7]

Libraries have employed some of these concepts already, like lifelong learning goals and employing various technologies. Not to be overlooked are the areas of STEM and STEAM. Let's define these two terms and discuss how the library has already been employing the concepts into its programming. "STEM stands for science, technology, engineering, and mathematics. The need for STEM programming in education developed out of concern that future generations were lacking critical skills needed to succeed in the current and future economy.

> STEM programming teaches innovation, creativity, critical thinking, problem solving and collaboration among many other skills proven to lead to success. STEAM embraces all the same elements but also adds a fifth element, specifically art. In this instance, arts ranges from visual arts, language arts, dance and physical arts, as well as music and more. STEAM focuses on sparking imagination and creativity through the arts in ways that naturally align with STEM learning.[8]

Early in my youth department librarianship career, around 2015, I first learned of STEM and STEAM and how libraries could support educational concepts by including them in programming. Such a cool idea! I was excited to embrace the trend and have watched it flourish over time; the most recent example of its inclusion is with an activity that will be outlined in the makerspace section. The Homemade Wigglebot program was held recently at my public library and utilized DC motors, red plastic cups, googly eyes, markers, wires, and a switch. If you're interested in this, it's easily found with a Google search, or better yet, seek out STEAM and STEM books that include multiple projects for your program planning.

By examining education trends, it's clear that libraries can mirror concepts to help support school curriculums. I would also encourage having conversations with teachers about how the library may act as a collaborator on specific elements of classwork; they will appreciate the interest, and it will forge/build upon a mutually beneficial alliance.

BUILDINGS: FLEXIBLE LEARNING SPACES

How will library space needs change over the next five to ten years? I'd like to begin by considering how library needs changed during Covid-19. Two major changes resulted from the pandemic. The first was a need for virtual or hybrid programming. It is quite conceivable that the near future will continue the trend of ensuring library programs provide connections to those who aren't able to come to the library in person. Having adequate resources to make this happen—a sound system, microphones, cameras, projector or large screen, and good Internet connections—is vital. The second major change was the need for outdoor space. Don't have an amphitheater? Not a problem! Portable plastic chairs and a flat open-grass area is all it takes to create a usable outdoor space. I've seen outdoor area usage invite so many possibilities for programming and connections. We recently partnered with the recreation department in our town to offer an early autumn outdoor showing of *Coco* in which families brought their picnic dinner and blankets and enjoyed a warm fall evening under the stars watching a film together. It was a beautiful bonding experience that brought together not only the patrons but also the recreation department staff and library staff in a positive and engaging atmosphere. In short, we all had fun!

Other considerations of future space needs come from understanding the changing needs of the youth and their families in our communities. When someone with vision and creativity examines a youth department's space and thinks critically about how kids will use the space, what is beneficial, and what is not—a revolution may occur! I've seen librarians transform what was once bland, generic, uninviting space into something kids cannot wait to visit because they feel seen, heard, honored, and welcome. Library youth departments of the future must explore the users' needs, and among the many current explorations is that of space flexibility, collaboration space, interactive displays, and dedicated group and quiet study areas.

Beginning with flexibility, I cannot sound the horn of gratitude loudly enough for bookcases on wheels! In mere moments, a room of book stacks becomes a performance area or a play area. Keeping this in mind will help maximize limited spaces and can ease up funds for those with budgetary constraints.

Makerspaces, or collaboration spaces, are a staple of the library youth department today. I can't tell you how much my nieces, ages seven and nine, loved the makerspace activity I brought to them from our public library's incredible youth librarian. They carefully put together their "wiggle bots" and then watched the little robot-like creature make art on a large sheet of paper. Communal creative space needs are simple and include tables to work on, supply storage, and, for more advanced needs, electronic and more technology related amenities for watching YouTube DIY videos or having a 3D printer. There are many resources available online to learn more about makerspace activities and tools, which I welcome the reader to explore. While many makerspaces are focused on teens, elementary-aged children should be included in this exciting creation adventure.

Book and other displays that employ interactive elements can also provide excitement in the public library. Kids may move a car along on a bulletin board every time they've read a book, and for older readers, they may post their latest favorite book's cover on a display; however an interactive display is created, it's sure to engage young library patrons providing them ownership of their space.

Finally, providing dedicated areas for both collaborative work as well as quiet spaces ensures that all users find areas that benefit them. Study carrels help students focus on homework, and large, centrally located tables provide the needed space to be creative during programs and stay-and-make activities.

LOOKING TO NON-LIBRARY INDUSTRIES FOR CLUES

I think of all the concepts that are presented here, one of the most fascinating and important is the idea that the library needs to think outside the literal and figurative "library box." Next time you walk into a Barnes & Noble, ask yourself, *How is the store drawing in their customers?* Looking to non-library business models in retail, and even restaurant concepts, can help the library innovate services, market itself effectively, focus more on the user-experience, increase efficiency, become more adaptable and innovative, and improve decision-making. Examining business strategies can help libraries better understand consumer needs and thereby adapt to meet the user "where they're at."

While much of what's in this chapter may be seen as current library practices, beginning with what is current can help inform the future. Final thoughts are to embrace change but cling to that which will benefit your community members. Thoroughly explore what is and what is not working in the library and adjust. Remaining current with trends impacting libraries is a quest and doesn't just "happen"—the librarian needs to understand the community they work in, actively engage with data and offerings, and may reject those things that don't serve their specific community, and that's okay. Adopting innovative concepts is great, but after trying them on, honestly examining whether they've improved library service or not, is the key to success.

REVIEW QUESTIONS

1. Seek out the book *Library NEXT: 7 Action Steps for Reinvention* by Catherine Murray-Rust and outline the seven steps. How do these steps for reinvention inform the future of libraries?
2. Explore demographic information for your area and report on your findings. Outline any surprises you've found. Will the information you discovered impact the work you're currently doing in the library? If you're not currently in a library, examine offerings on your local library's website and outline whether the programming you discover meets the needs of the demographic population you've learned about.
3. Think about meaningful connections you've made in your life. How important do you think it is to provide these kinds of connections with library pa-

trons? Outline some instances that you've had with patrons that show how important these connections with patrons can be; if you're not currently in a library, seek out some research or interview a librarian at your local library about their thoughts on interacting in this way with library patrons.
4. Looking at your local library, in what ways does programming for children reflect educational trends, and what educational trends do you find in the library's programming?
5. Create at least two ways that a non-library business's practices for attracting and keeping customers could benefit the library with marketing.
6. To consider the future of libraries, think about your local library by looking at the past and how it has (or hasn't) evolved over time. Outline several instances that reflect ways the library has changed to meet patron needs.

NOTES

1. Catherine Murray-Rust, *Library NEXT: 7 Action Steps for Reinvention* (Chicago: ALA Editions, 2021), v.
2. Ibid.
3. Michael Stephens, *Whole-Hearted Librarianship: Finding Hope, Inspiration, and Balance* (Chicago: ALA Editions, 2019), 41.
4. Medium: EveryLibrary, "Libraries are a Gateway to Community Connection: Making Small Connections at your Library can Have Profound Effects on Your Life and the Lives of Your Neighbors," accessed December 2, 2023, https://medium.com/everylibrary/libraries-are-a-gateway-to-community-connection-6fd909b16037.
5. Stephens, *Whole-Hearted Librarianship*, 59.
6. Charla Viera, "5 Ways Artificial Intelligence Impacts Libraries," accessed December 2, 2023, https://www.aje.com/arc/ways-artificial-intelligence-impacts-libraries/.
7. Eric Debétaz, "Top Education Trends to Watch in 2024," accessed December 2, 2023, https://hospitalityinsights.ehl.edu/education-trends.
8. 50 Years National Inventors Hall of Fame, "The STEM vs. STEAM Debate," accessed December 2, 2023, https://www.invent.org/blog/trends-stem/stem-steam-defined/.

Index

33 Winning Summer Reading Program Ideas, 72
5 Marketing Strategies to Promote Your Library, 137
5 Steps of Outcome-Based Planning & Evaluation for Youth Services, 26, 28, 124

About Books, Children, and Libraries, 7
Accelerated Reader, 70
accessibility, 99, 101–2; assessment of, 107–8; library building and, 106
ACLU. See American Civil Liberties Union
ACPL. See Allen County Public Library
Adkins, Denice, 107
"Adventure Begins at Your Library," 64
Advocacy Toolkit: The Importance and Purpose of Library Advocacy, 126
advocacy: budgets and funding and, 132–33; children's services and, 124–26; definition of, 124
AI. See artificial intelligence
ALA Round Table on Work with Negroes, 5
ALA. See American Library Association
ALA's "Virtual Storytimes Services Guide," 56
ALA's Code of Ethics, 118
Allen County (IN) Public Library (ACPL), 28
The Alliance of Justice, 124
Allison, Michael, 22, 23
ALSC. See Association for Library Service to Children
ALSC's Championing Children's Services Toolkit, 125–26
ALSC's Disability Awareness Training, 110
American Civil Liberties Union, 114
The American Community Survey, 107
American Disabilities Act of 1990, 106

"American Indians in Children's Literature," 87
American Indian Literature Award, 94
American Libraries Magazine, 139
American Library Association (ALA) Annual Conference, 94
American Library Association (ALA), 4, 7, 26, 72, 86, 87, 94, 105, 114, 115, 118, 122, 139
American Library Association store, 139
American Library Association's (ALA) Adult Education Roundtable, 77
Amos: The Story of an Old Dog and His Couch, 41
The Amulet of Samarkand, 116
And Tango Makes Three, 116
Anderson, Amelia, 107
Andrew Heiskell Braille, 108
Anne Frank: The Diary of a Young Girl, 116
Arnold, Lillian, 3
artificial intelligence, 149
Asana, 23
assistive amplification reading software, 108
assistive technologies, types of, 108; Andrew Heiskell Braille, 108; assistive amplification software, 108; closed-circuit television enlargers, 108; Duxbury Braille Translation Software, 108; Kurzweil 1000 Scanning and Reading Software, 108; nonvisual desktop access (NVDA), 108; personal reading machines, 108; Talking Book Library, 108; Talking Typing Teacher, 108
Association for Library Service to Children (ALSC): Championing Children's Services Toolkit, 125–27; Competencies for Librarians Serving

155

Children in Libraries, 10, 122-24; Curiosity Creates grant, 10
Atlanta-Fulton (GA) Public Library, 6
Australian College of Applied Professions, 131
autism spectrum, 107
awards, children's literature: Caldecott Award, 94; Flume: New Hampshire Teen Reader's Choice Award, 139; Newbery Award, 94; New Hampshire Great Stone Face Book Award, 94, 139; Printz Award, 94; Pura Belpré Award, 7; Stonewall Awards, 94; Walter Dean Meyers Award, 94

"Bad Guys Doing Good," 53
Baby Bouncers, 46
Baby Jamboree, 46
baby lapsit program, 45
The Baby Tree, 116
baby yoga program, 52
Baker, Lynn, 14, 15
banned books: banned books book club, 117; banned books week, 115; definition of, 114-15
Bark, George (book), 39
Bark, George and More Doggie Tales (visual material), 39
Barnes and Noble, 152
Bay Area Discovery Museum, 10
beading program, 54
Beanstack, 70
"Becoming Age Friendly," 108
Belpré, Pura, 7
Benesch, Amber, 102
Bequest of Wings, 7
Berkner, Laurie, 35, 39, 40
Berman, Sandy, 104
Best Team Ever!: The Surprising Science of High-Performing Teams, 131
Better Nate Than Never, 115
big books, 42
Black Boy, 5
Black History Month, 105
Blue, Thomas Fountain, 5
Bogan, Kelsey, 90-91, 104-5
boltjobs.com, 127
book challenges, 86

books challenges, 114; lists of, 115; middle-grade title list of, 116; picture book title list of, 116
The Book with No Pictures, 48
Boston (MA) Public Library, 4
Boy Toy, 116
branding, library marketing, 135
Bratt, Jessica, 50
The Bridge to Terebithia, 116
Brooklyn (NY) Pratt Institute, 2, 4
Brown Bear, Brown Bear, What Do You See?, 42
Brown v. Board of Education, 6
Brown, Nancy, 77
Brown, Peter, 80
Brown, Stuart, 44
budgets, library, 132-35; how to create, 133; Maine Library Trustee Handbook and, 133-34
building flexibility, library, 150-51
Burkus, David, 131
Burnite, Caroline, 4
Bushman, Bobbie, 107
business strategies, 152

Caldecott Award, 94
call and response technique, 14
Calvert, Philip, 26
Campana, et.al., 13
Canva, 128
Carnegie Library of Pittsburg, 4, 128
Carnegie, Andrew, 6
Cassell, Kay Ann, 81, 82, 124
cataloging, library: accepted terminology, 109; diverse representation in, 104
censorship, 113-18; censorship, and state laws, 116; definition of, 114; diverse books and, 103; self-censorship, 85-87; soft censorship, 86
Champaign (IL) Library, 3, 4
charitable donations, 134
Charlie and the Great Glass Elevator, 80
Charlotte's Web, 80
"Checklist: Engaging Library Spaces for Children," 102
Chicago (IL) Public Library, 2

childhood development, 11-14; division of ages and, 122; five stages of, 11-12; foundation of, 11
Children and Libraries, 125
Children's Book Council, ALA, 87
children's librarianship, five laws of, 122
Children's Medical Centre, 11
children's programming: all-inclusive, 146; definition of, 8-9; foundational elements, 22; guidelines, 9; keys to success, 10; multiple formats, benefits of, 55-56; outdoor space, and, 151; planning with the result in mind, 51; policy, 9; programming, general, 51-55; self-assessment of, 51; value of, 8; virtual, 56-57
Children's Services, 87-88
children's services: brief history, 2; early development, 2-5
Christian Advocate, 2
Civil Rights Act of 1964, 6
clarity in management and leadership, 129, 130
Clark, Barbara, 6
Cleary, Beverly, 80
closed-circuit television enlargers, 108
CLSP. See Collaborative Summer Library Program
Code of Ethics, ALA, 82
cognitive disabilities, definition of, 107
collaborations: community, 148-49; teachers and, 150
Collaborative Summer Library Program (CSLP), 64, 72
collection development: analysis of, 88; building and maintaining, 87-88; diversity audit, 87-88; diversity, and 146; intellectual freedom and, 117; knowledge of community and, 85; policy, 86-87; race and ethnicity and, 146; self-censorship and, 85; weeding and, 84-93
collection development resources: "American Indians in Children's Literature," 87; Children's Book Council, ALA, 87; Cooperative Children's Book Center, 87; The Horn Book, 87; "I'm Here, I'm Queer, What the Hell Do I Read?," 87; Lee & Low Books, 87; School Library Journal, 87; "We Need Diverse Books," 87
Collection Management for Youth: Equity, Inclusion, and Learning, 88
collection shelving, 88-91; bookstore/retail model, 89-90; dynamic, 88-89, 90-91; genrefying, 89
Colorado Department of Education, 62
commitment in management and leadership, 129, 131
community center, library as, 137, 145
community demographics, 146
community engagement, 148-49
compassion in management and leadership, 129, 130
The Complete Collections Assessment Manual: A Holistic Approach, 88
Competencies for Librarians Serving Children in Libraries, 122, 124
connection in management and leadership, 129; need for in workplace, 131
Constant Contact, 127-28
Continuous Review, Evaluation, and Weeding. See CREW
Cooperative Children's Book Center, 87
core competencies, children/youth librarians, 121, 122-24
Covid-19: digital preparedness and, 128; space needs and, 66, 150; virtual programming and 56
Crash Course in Children's Programming, 110, 136
Crazy 8s Math Club, 52
creativity, components critical to, 10
CREW: A Weeding Manual for Modern Libraries, 92
Crow, Sherry, 16

Dahl, Roald, 80
deaccession. See weeding
Debétaz, Eric, 149
Demco: dynamic shelving and, 90; space planning and, 102; summer reading resource, 72
demographic trends, 146-47
Dewey Decimal System, 105

dialogic reading: defined, 13-14; four elements of, 14; PEER sequence, 14
Diamant-Cohen, Betsy, 44, 45, 138
digital integration, 149
The Digital Library of America, 6
digital media literacy, 15. See also multiliteracy
digital preparedness, 126-29; perpetual beta, 127; technological competency, 127
digital tools, everyday applications: Canva, 128; Constant Contact, 127-28
"A Dirty Little Secret: Self-Censorship is Rampant and Lethal," 116
disabilities, children with: accessibility for, 102, 107-8; assessment of materials for, 109; assessment of space for, 107; cognitive, 107; developmental, 107; inclusivity of, 109; intellectual, 107; issues raised in literature, 109; non-visual, 107; outreach and partnerships, 110-11; programming for, 106-9; resources for, 107; sensory sensitivity of, 108-9; staff training in, 110; surveying community, 111
Disability Horizons website, 109
diverse literature, 104
diverse populations, 147
diverse representation, 104-5
diversity: blogs, 124; outreach and development and, 106; professional development and, 106
The Diversity Factor: Igniting Superior Organizational Performance, 106
Donaldson, Julia, 38, 40
donations, source of library funding, 134
"Don't Shush Me: Adventures of a 21st Century High School Librarian," 90, 140
Drag Story Hour, 49-50; defined, 49; history of, 49; opposition to, 50
Drama, 116
Dubois, W.E.B., 6
Duff, Annis, 7
Duluth (MN) Public Library, 4
Duxbury Braille Translation Software, 108

dynamic shelving: defined, 90; drawbacks, 91; weeding, and, 92

early literacy: defined, 12; model of, 12; value of, 11-14
earlylit.net, 13
EBSCO, 139
EBSCO Connect, 134
ECRR. See Every Child Ready to Read
The Electric Company, 6
encyclopedia.com, 3
engagement: baby storytime and, 43-44; benefits of, 148; collaborations and, 148-49; family storytime and, 49; interactive space and, 102; marketing and, 108-9; outreach and, 106; programming in multiple formats and, 56; social literacy and, 15; storytime and, 36-37, 40; strategic planning and, 24; toddler storytime and, 46
enrichment, library programming, 55-56
equal access in libraries, poor, 5-7
equity, diversity, inclusion, and belonging, in the library, 99; representation and, 104-5; space planning and, 102
Evaluating a Public Library Makerspace, 26
Evans, Edward G., 129, 130, 133, 135
Every Child Ready to Read Depends on Libraries Preparing Parents for Lifelong Learning Involvement in Literacy, 13
Every Child Ready to Read Initiative, 12-13; caregiver education in, 13; family-centric approach, 13; six literacy skills of, 12
"Everyday Advocacy: Doing What You Do," 125-26
Everywhere Babies, 116
Exemplary Children's Programming: An Initiative, 10-11

The Family Book, 116
Farmer, Leslie, 125
Fasick, Adele, 9, 55, 127
Fathauer, Elizabeth, 3
Feiffer, Jules, 39
Filoque L'Heure Joyeuse, 4

findability, diverse representation and, 104
fingerplay, defined, 39
Fitzgerald, Katie, 36
"Five Little Monkeys Jumping on the Bed," 39
flannel boards, defined, 42
Florida State University, 29
The Flume: New Hampshire Teen Reader's Choice Award, 139
focus book, defined, 39
Foundations in Intellectual Freedom, 114
founding mothers, 7-8
the "four Cs," 129-31
Freda, Cecilia, 124
Frederickson, Barbara, 44
Freedom to Read Statement, 87
Friends of the Library groups, 63, 67, 71, 83, 132, 134
Fundamentals of Children's Services, 139
funding, library, 132-35; budgets and, 132-35; charitable donations, 134; disability programming and, 107; EBSCO Connect, 134; Friends of the Library, 134; gifts, 134; grants, 134; IMLS, 134; outreach and, 137; program creation and, 68; Project Outcome and, 27; resources, 63, 134; strategic plan and, 24; wish list, 134-35

Gahagan, Pia, 26
Gardner, Howard, 45
Garrisons, Star Wars 53
George, 116
Ghoting, Saraj Nadkarni, 13, 43
gifts and donations, library funding, 134
Gillespie, Katie, 50
goals, library, 136-37
"Goodbye Friends," 41
Goodreads, 78, 79, 115
Gower, Stephen, 102
Grand Rapids (MI) Public Library, 50
grants: funding, 134; resources, 134
Graves, Marjorie, 3
Greenwell, Stacey, 129
Gross, Melissa, 21, 26, 28, 29, 30, 31, 124
The Gruffalo, 39

Hadini, Helen, 10
Hannaford, Carla, 45
Harry Potter Club program, 52
"Harry Potter in 99 Seconds," 35
Harry Potter series, 116
Hearne, Betsy, 7
"Hello Friends," 38
Hensley, Daniel, 28
Higgins, Susan, 135
Hiremath, Uma, 82
Holt, Leslie Edmonds, 9, 55, 127
homework help, 83-84
homework cart, 83
Hoopla, 149
The Horn Book, 87, 124, 139
Hoskin, Ellen, 116
Houde, Lisa, 124
"How to Have Difficult Conversations," 106
Hughes-Hassel, Sandra, 88

I am Jazz, 116
IFLA. See International Federation of Library Associations and Institutions
Illinois Library Association, 126
"I'm Here, I'm Queer, What the Hell Do I Read?," 87
IMLS. See Institute of Museum and Library Services
Impactful Community-Based Literacy Projects, 125
"inching up the ramp," 122
in loco parentis, 87
In Our Mothers' House, 116
inclusive language, in the library, 105-6
inclusivity, 109
indeed.com, 130
indie publishers, 124
Inspiring a Generation to Create: Critical Components of Creativity in Children, 10
Institute of Museum and Library Services (IMLS), 29, 134
intellectual disabilities, 107
Intellectual Freedom Manual, 86, 113
intellectual freedom: definition of, 113; library services, and 113-14; Pat Scales and, 117; policies and procedures,

Index 159

117-18; resources for, 113-14; staff training in, 117
interactive songs, 40
interactive storytime model, 37
International Federation of Library Associations and Institutions (IFLA), 16
International Youth Library in Munich, 4
iREAD, 64

Jaegar, Garret, 10
jbrary.com, 37, 140
Jenkins, Christine, 7
Jennison, Anne, 56
Jensen, Kelly, 86
Jim Crow South, 5, 6
Johnson (KS) County Library, 12
Juan Bobo and the Queen's Necklace, 7

Kelly, Madeline, 88
King, Stephen, 115
Klatt, Kathy Fling, 43
Knox, Emily, 114
Kurzweil 1000 Scanning and Reading Software, 108

l8r, g8r, 116
Lambert, Meagan Dowd, 37
LaRue, James, 117, 118, 123
leadership: definition of, 130; twenty qualities of, 130
Lee & Low Books, 87
Lee, Robert Ellis, 77
Lego Club program, 53
Lego Harry Potter Hogwarts Castle program, 53
Lesbian, Gay, Bisexual, Transgender, Queer/Questioning, Intersex, Asexual, Two-Spirit Teens. See LGBTQIA2S+ Teens
Let's Talk About Race in Storytimes, 50
LGBTQIA2S+ Teens, 102-4
LGBTQIA2S+ young adult literature book challenges, 115
Libby, 149
Library League of children, 3
Library Next: 7 Action Steps for Reinvention, 145

Library of Congress, 104-5, 109
LibraryThing, 78, 79
lifelong learning: administration, children's services and, 121; definition of, 16, 105-6; development and value of, 16; diverse representation and, 105; early literacy and, 13; educational trends and, 150; family storytime and, 49; management and leadership and, 129; mission statement and, 22; outreach and marketing and, 137; professional development and, 106; programming in multiple formats and, 55; Rye Public Library and, 16, 22, 136
Lindgren, Astrid, 80
Little Listeners, 46
Living Dead Girl, 85, 116
LOC. See Library of Congress
Lock-in program, 53
Loewecke, Angela, 102
Lonigan, Christopher, 12
Loop, Karis, 122
Lord, Cynthia, 109
Los Angeles (CA) Public Library, 6
Lyga, Barry, 116

Maine Library Trustee Handbook, 133-34
makerspace: educational trends and, 150; enrichment programs and, 56; flexible learning spaces and, 151; outreach and marketing and, 135; professional development and, 139; reporting and, 26
management and leadership, 129-31; resources for, 131
Management Basics for Information Professionals, fourth edition, 129
Management Basics for Information Professionals, second edition, 130, 133-35
Managing Children's Services in Libraries, 9
marketing, library, 135-37; benefits of, 137; campaign, 137; children's services advocacy, 124; dynamic shelving and, 90; library goals and, 136; library promotion and, 137; outreach and, 135-37; professional development

and, 121; programming in multiple formats and, 55; programming, children's, 9; storytime and, 41
Materials for Young Adults, 123, 128
Matthew Effect, 12
Maus, 115
May Institute, 107, 110
May the 4th Be with You program, 53
Mayo Clinic, 128
McKim, Jr., James T., 106
mclskids.pbworks.com, 46
Media Mentorship in Libraries Serving Youth, 127
Mediavilla, Cindy, 21, 26, 28, 29-31, 124
Medium, 147-48
Memphis (TN) Public Library, 5
mentor, library, 139-40
MGOL. See Mother Goose on the Loose
mgol.net, 44
midnight walking tacos, 35
"A Midsummer Night's Dream," 57
Minneapolis (MN) Public Library, 2
mission statement: administration and, 121; budgets and funding and, 132; collection development policy and, 87; commitment to, 129; definition of, 22; "four Cs" and, 129; library, 22-23; management and leadership and, 131; marketing and, 136-37; Rye Public Library, 16, 121; strategic planning and, 24-25; virtual programming and, 57
mobile bookcases, 101, 151
Moore, Anne Carroll, 2, 4, 7
Mother Goose on the Loose (MOGL): baby storytime and, 43; eight intelligences, 45; method of, 43-46; nine teaching elements, 44; professional development and, 138
Movie Marathon program, 54
Moyers, Jessica, 78
Mrs. Frisby and the Rats of NIMH, 80
multiliteracy, 14-16; definition of, 14; digital media literacy and, 15; five modes of, 14-15; multisensory literacy and, 15; origin of, 14; social literacy and, 15; textual literacy and, 15; visual literacy and, 15

multisensory literacy, 15. See also multiliteracy
Murray-Rust, Catherine, 145
MUSTIE, weeding guideline, 92-93
My Road to Childhood, 7

NAACP Youth Council. See National Association for the Advancement of Colored People
The Name Jar, 116
Nard, Rachel, 128
National Archives at Boston, 82
National Association for the Advancement of Colored People (NAACP) Youth Council, 6
National Impact of Library Public Programs Assessment (NILPPA), 55
Native Son, 5
neurodiversity, 107
New England Collaborative Summer Summit, 72
New Hampshire Great Stone Face Award, 94, 139
New Hampshire Library Association, 126
New Hampshire State Library, 64
A New Inquisition: Understanding and Managing Intellectual Freedom Challenges, 117, 123
New Jersey State Library, 137
New Kid, 116
New London Group, 14, 15
New York (NY) Public Library, 7; aassistive technology and, 108; Brainfuze, 84; Jackson Heights, 50
The New York Times bestseller list, 124
Newbery Award, 94
Nikki, 116
NILPPA. See National Impact of Library Public Programs Assessment
No More Static Shelves! Making Your Collection More Dynamic and Less Daunting, 88
non-library industries, business strategies of, 152
nonvisual desktop access (NVDA), 108
noodle storytime, 35
Novelist Plus, 80
NVDA. See nonvisual desktop access

O'Brien, Robert, 80
OBPE. See outcome-based planning and evaluation
Ogle, Rebecca, 56, 57
Olcott, Francis Jenkins, 4
Olive's Ocean, 116
"On Censorship," 117
organizationalignition.com, 106
outcome-based planning and evaluation (OBPE): key elements of, 26–27; methods of, 21; program planning and, 21; youth services, 28–29
outdoor space, 151
outreach: administration and, 121; benefits of, 136; children's disabilities and, 106–7; diversity and, 106; funding resources, 63, 137; historical perspective of, 2; marketing and, 135–37; outcome-based planning and evaluation project, 29; partnerships and, 135–36; program creation and, 68; publicity, promotion and, 69; school-aged storytime and, 48; staff training in, 110–11; welcoming and inclusive library, 99

partnerships: budgets and funding and, 133; outreach and, 110–11, 135–37; program planning in multiple formats and, 55; Project Outcome and, 28
pandemic, 25, 56, 67, 91, 128, 147, 149, 150
Part of Our Lives: A People's History of the American Public Library, 2, 7
Pax, 80
PBS. See Public Broadcasting Service
Peck, Penny, 110, 136
pedagogy, 14
Pen America, 116
Perez and Martina, 7
personal reading machines, 108
Pew Research Data, 1
"Pig on Her Head," 39
Pink, Daniel, 131
Pinterest, 41, 57, 101
Pippi Longstocking, 80
PLA. See Public Library Association
Plessy v. Ferguson, 6

Plummer, Mary Wright, 2
Polikoff, Morgan, 62
Potter, Beatrix, 80
Pride Month, 105
Pride: The Story of Harvey Milk and the Rainbow Flag, 116
Printz Award, 94
Professional Development Harvard Division of Continuing Education, 138
professional development: award committees and, 138; beyond the library exploration, 140; blogs and, 140; conferences and, 138; definition of, 138; engagement and, 138; jbrary and, 140; librarians, 137–41; library listservs and, 140; writing, speaking & teaching, 140
professional ethics, 118
program examples: Baby Yoga 52; Beading, 54; Crazy 8s Math Club, 52; Harry Potter Club, 52; Lego Club, 53; Lego Harry Potter Hogwarts Castle, 53; Lock-In, 53; May the 4th Be with You, 53; Movie Marathon, 54; Teen Advisory Board, 53
Project CATE, 29
Project Gutenberg, 93
Project Outcome, 21; conducting evaluations, 30–31; determining outcomes, 30; developing programs and services, 30; development of, 26; gathering information, 29–30; impact survey, 27–28; impacts of, 28; in action, 28; leveraging the library's role, 31; site, 27; toolkit, 27–28
Promoting Your Library: Getting the Message Out, 124
Public Broadcasting Service (PBS), 86
Public Libraries and Their Communities, 124
Public Libraries Online, 28
Public Library Association, 26
Pulitzer Prize, 115
Pura Belpré Award, 7

qualitative data, 25; public library reporting of, 25–26

quantitative data, 25; public library reporting of, 25–26
quiet censorship, 86
Quinn, David, 62

racial and religious targeting, 103
racism and bias, in cataloging, 105
Radiant Child: The Story of Young Artist Jean-Michel Basquiat, 116
radical cataloging, 104
Raffi, 40
Ramona Forever, 80
Rand, Mary Tuck, 16, 23
Ranganathan's Five Laws of Librarianship, 122
Reader's Theatre, 57
Readers' Advisory Services in the Public Library, 77
readers' advisory, 75–80; caregivers and, 80; defined, 76; history of, 77; reference interviews and, 75; tips and tricks, 78–80
reading enhancement programs, 55, 56
Reading Picture books with Children: How to Shake Up Storytime and Get Kids Talking About What They See, 37
Reading Rockets, 14
reading tracking apps: Accelerated Reader, 70; Beanstack, 70; READsquared, 70
READsquared, 70
Real-World Teen Services, 99
reference interview: core competencies and, 123; defined, 81–83; history of, 77; how to perform, 82–83; readers' advisory and, 75–76
reference services: basics of, 82–83; definition of, 81–82; history of, 81
refuge, library as a place of, 104
resource-sharing, 135
Rizzo, Nicholas, 1
The Rocky Horror Picture Show, 54
Rogalla, Mike, 3
ROI Calculator, 126
Romp and Rhyme, 46
Room on the Broom, 38
Rosie Walks, 42

RPL. See Rye Public Library
Rules, 109
Ruscio, Erica, 125
Rye Public Library: administration and, 121; lifelong learners and, 16, 136; mission statement of, 22; program evaluation and, 22; reporting in libraries and, 28; strategic plan of, 24; vision statement of, 23

Sacred Texts: What Our Foremothers Left Us in the Way of Psalms, Proverbs, Precepts, and Practices, 8
safe space, library, 103
San Francisco (CA) Public Library, 107
San José State University, 90, 124, 147
Saricks, Joyce, 77
Sawyer, Ethel, 6
Sayers, Frances Clark, 7
scaffolding, defined, 43
Scales, Pat, 117
Scholastic Video Collection, 39
School Library Journal, 71, 87, 117, 124, 139
Science, Technology, Engineering, and Mathematics, 139, 149–50; definition of, 150
Science, Technology, Engineering, Art, and Mathematics, 139, 149–50; definition of, 150
Scott, Elizabeth, 85, 116
Seacoast Outright, 135
Seamless Youth Services for Every Age and Stage, 122
self-censorship, 85–86, 115–17
sense of belonging in the library, 99
sensitivity and respect in the library, 105–6
sensory sensitivity, 108–9
Separate is Never Equal, 116
Serving LGBTQ Teens: A Practical Guide for Librarians, 103–4
Sesame Street, 6
Sing a Song, 116
Singer, Judy, 107
sit-ins, library, 6
social connections, 147–48
social literacy, 15. See also multiliteracy

Index   **163**

soft censorship, 86
Southern California Garrison, 53
space needs, 150
space planning, library: age-appropriate areas, 101-2; color, 99-100; décor and comfort, 100-101; equity, diversity, inclusion and belonging, 102-6; interactive, 102; safety, 101-2; self-assessment checklist, 100; space needs, 100; surveying, 100; transforming, 101
Sparkle Boy, 116
Spiegelman, Art, 115
St. Louis (MO) Public Library, 29
State Library of New Hampshire, 25. See also New Hampshire State Library
state library-sponsored performer showcase, 65, 67
static shelving, 90
STEAM. See Science, Technology, Engineering, Art, and Mathematics
Stella Brings the Family, 116
STEM. See Science, Technology, Engineering, and Mathematics
Stephens, Michael, 147, 148-49
Stick Man, 38
Stonewall Awards, 94
Stormtroopers, 53
Storytime Success: A Practical Guide for Librarians, 36
storytime, 36-51; anti-oppression framework in, 50; basic structure, 38; birth to age five, 42; defined, 36; elements, 38; family, 48-49; babies, 43; names, 46; non-hearing children, 109; ground rules, 39; movement activities, 40-41; musts, 37-38; planning for fun, 38; planning of, 36-37; preschool, 47-48; race included in, 50; school-aged, 48; study, 13; tips for successful, 42; toddler, 46-47. See also Mother Goose on the Loose
Stover, Katie, 78
strategic plan, library, 24-25; collection development and, 85; future in libraries and, 145; program evaluation and, 21; Project Outcome and, 28-29; virtual programming and, 57

Streisand, Barbara, 147
Sullivan, Michael, 87, 139
Sulwe, 116
summer learning loss, 61-62
summer math slide, 62
summer reading program: assessing venues, 66; considering space needs, 66; displays, 68; donations to, 71; evaluation of, 71; funding resources, 63, 67; hiring performers, 66-67; incentives, 70-71; lack of budget, 67; "library bucks," 68, 71; magicians, 67; measurement options, 69-70; non-reading activities, 70; organization and planning of, 62-63; planning dates and times, 65-66; prizes, 71; program creation, 68; promotion, 68, 69; reading encouragement, 68; resources for, 72-73; school visit, 69; theme options, 64-65; tracking process, 69-70; why create, 61; wildlife rescue organizations, 67
summer reading program passive programs: guessing jar, 68; make-and-take craft kits, 68; scavenger hunts, 68; themed mazes, 68; trivia, 68
Summer Reading Program Resources LibGuide, 72
summer slide, 61-62
Summoned by Books, 7
The Supernaturalist, 116

The Tale of Peter Rabbit, 80
Talking Book Library, 108
Talking Typing Machnine, 108
Tea, Michelle, 49
technology: children, impacts on, 128; children's programming and, 128; Mayo Clinic and, 128
Teen Advisory Board program, 53
Texas State Library and Archive Commission, 92
textual literacy, 15. See also multiliteracy
They, She, He Easy as ABC, 116
Tolin, Lisa, 116
"Top 10 Skills Every Librarian Needs to Succeed in Today's Digital World," 127

"Top Education Trends to Watch For in 2024," 149
Totally Joe, 116
trends, educational, 149–50

U.S. Department of Education, 62
University of Illinois, 3
University of Washington Information School, 27–28

value statement, library, 21, 22
Velásquez, Jennifer, 99
"the vanishing time," 122
The Very Hungry Caterpillar, 42
"Victor Vito," 35
Viera, Charla, 149
Viguer, Ruth Hill, 7
virtual services, 149
Virtual Storytimes, 56
vision statement, library, 23–24; outcome-based planning and programming and, 29; programming in multiple formats and, 56; purpose of, 22; virtual programs and, 57
visual literacy, 15. See also multiliteracy
Vnuk, Rebecca, 91, 93
Von Letkemann, Lucia, 88–89, 91
Voting Rights Act of 1965, 6

walking tacos, vii
Walt Disney Company, 10
Walter Dean Meyers Award, 94
Walter, Virginia A., 2, 21, 26, 28, 29, 30, 31, 122, 124
Ward, Patricia, 130, 133, 135
We are Grateful, 116
We March, 116
"We Need Diverse Books," 87, 124

weeding, 91–93: CREW method of, 92; gaps in the collection and, 92; MUSTIE guidelines of, 92; outdated materials and, 92; space management and, 92
The Weeding Handbook: A Shelf-by-Shelf Guide, 91
What the Ladybug Heard, 40
whatshouldireadnext.com, 80
Whelan, Debra, 116
When Aiden Became a Brother, 116
whimsylibrarian.com, 50
White Bird, 116
Whitehurst, Grover, 12, 14
whole book approach, 37
Whole-Hearted Librarianship: Finding Hope, Inspiration, and Balance, 147
A Whole New Mind: Why Right-Brainers Will Rule the Future, 131
Wichita (KS) Public Library, 8, 9
Wiegand, Wayne A., 2, 7
wigglebot, 150
Wikipedia, 49, 76, 81, 113
Wildlife Encounters, 67
The Wild Robot, 80
Willems, Mo, 91
"Winter Tales with Anne Jennison," 56
wish list, library funding, 134
Work Smarter, Not Harder, 28
Worm Loves Worm, 116
Wright, Richard, 5

youth media awards, 94
Youth Services and Public Libraries, 135

Zoom, 56
Zoombombing, 57

About the Author

Lisa Houde is the assistant director and collection development and interlibrary loan manager at the Rye Public Library in Rye, New Hampshire. She holds a BA in liberal arts from Seattle University and an MLIS from San José State University. Lisa also teaches multiple graduate courses in Library and Information Science at San José State University's iSchool, including Programming and Services for Children, Materials for Young Adults, Seminar in Contemporary Issues—Graphic Novels (young adult focus), and Resources and Information Services in Professions and Disciplines—LGBTIQ Resources and Services. Lisa is a member of the New Hampshire Library Association (NHLA) as well as the American Library Association. In the NHLA, Lisa is a past president of Young Adult Library Services of New Hampshire (YALS) and has presented at conferences on library services to LGBTQIA2S+ teens, as well as presenting nominated title book talks for the NHLA Flume Teen Readers' Choice Award, having served on that committee for several years. Lisa has also served on the NHLA Great Stone Face Book Award committee and presented those titles at conferences as well. Lisa was fortunate to serve on the American Library Association's Gay, Lesbian, Bisexual and Transgender Roundtable (GLBTRT) Advisory Committee and was one of the authors of the GLBTRT toolkit "Open to All: Service the GLBT Community in Your Library." Finally, Lisa authored a previous title on serving LGBTQIA2S+ teens, *Serving LGBTQ Teens: A Practical Guide for Librarians* (2018).

www.ingramcontent.com/pod-product-compliance
Lightning Source LLC
Chambersburg PA
CBHW031710230426
43668CB00006B/176